Small Teaching K–8

Small Teaching K–8

Igniting the Teaching Spark with the Science of Learning

Sarah Connell Sanders
James M. Lang

JB JOSSEY-BASS™
A Wiley Brand

Published by Jossey-Bass

A Wiley Brand
111 River St., Hoboken NJ 07030
www.josseybass.com

Printed in the United States of America
Published simultaneously in Canada

Jossey-Bass books and products are available through most bookstores. To contact Jossey-Bass directly call our Customer Care Department within the U.S. at 800-956-7739, outside the U.S. at 317-572-3986, or fax 317-572-4002.

Wiley publishes in a variety of print and electronic formats and by print-on-demand. Some material included with standard print versions of this book may not be included in e-books or in print-on-demand. If this book refers to media such as a CD or DVD that is not included in the version you purchased, you may download this material at http://booksupport.wiley.com. For more information about Wiley products, visit www.wiley.com.

Library of Congress Cataloging-in-Publication Data.

Names: Sanders, Sarah Connell, author. | Lang, James M., author. |
Jossey-Bass Inc., publisher.
Title: Small teaching K–8 : igniting the teaching spark with the science of learning
/ Sarah Connell Sanders, James M. Lang.
Description: Hoboken, NJ : Jossey-Bass, [2023] | Includes bibliographical
references and index.
Identifiers: LCCN 2022023672 (print) | LCCN 2022023673 (ebook) | ISBN
9781119862796 (paperback) | ISBN 9781119863526 (adobe pdf) | ISBN
9781119863519 (epub)
Subjects: LCSH: Cognitive learning. | Education, Elementary—Research. |
Thought and thinking—Study and teaching.
Classification: LCC LB1062 .S3124 2023 (print) | LCC LB1062 (ebook) | DDC
370.15/23—dc23/eng/20220706
LC record available at https://lccn.loc.gov/2022023672
LC ebook record available at https://lccn.loc.gov/2022023673

Cover Design: Wiley
Author Photo by Michael Hendrickson

SKY10036407_100422

Contents

About the Authors

Sarah Connell Sanders has been a public school educator in Massachusetts for 13 years. She is currently the library media specialist at Burncoat Middle School in Worcester where she teaches in the gifted and talented program and spearheads community partnerships. In addition to her credentials as a school librarian, she is also a certified elementary teacher and secondary English teacher. She recently received her middle school Principal's License from the Massachusetts Department of Elementary and Secondary Education. Her credentials include a B.A. English and Education from Fordham University, an M. Ed. Curriculum and Instruction from Boston College, and an M. Ed. School Leadership and Administration from Worcester State University.

James M. Lang, Ph.D., is the author of six books, the most recent of which are *Small Teaching: Everyday Lessons from the Science of Learning* (2nd ed., 2021), *Distracted: Why Students Can't Focus and What You Can Do About It* (2020), and *Cheating Lessons: Learning from Academic Dishonesty* (2013). Lang writes a monthly column on teaching and learning for *The Chronicle of Higher Education*. He has conducted workshops on teaching for faculty at more than two hundred schools, colleges or universities in the United States and abroad, and consulted for the United Nations on the development of teaching materials in ethics and integrity in education. He has a B.A. in English and Philosophy from the University of Notre Dame, an M.A. in English from St. Louis University, and a Ph.D. in English from Northwestern University. You can follow him on Twitter at @LangOnCourse or learn more at http://jamesmlang.com.

Foreword

Since the original *Small Teaching* appeared in the fall of 2016, its two simple premises have been embraced by teachers around the world. The first premise is that we can improve the learning, personal development, and well-being of our students by paying attention to the small choices we make as we are designing learning experiences for them. The second premise is that those small choices will have the greatest impact if they are informed by current research on how human beings learn. Put those two premises together, and you have a program designed to improve education on an everyday scale, without the need for massive investments of time and money, or without falling into the trap of mindlessly embracing the latest fad in educational theory or educational technology.

The original book was intended for teachers in the physical classrooms of higher education, where I have spent most of my career. But the applicability of its core principles to the online classroom was apparent to a veteran of online teaching, Flower Darby, who approached me a few years ago with the proposal to co-author the book's first sequel, *Small Teaching Online*. That book appeared just before the pandemic hit in March of 2020, at a time that teachers everywhere were suddenly confronted with the challenge of teaching online, many for the first time. Flower had written a terrific book (with just a little help from me), which meant that *Small Teaching Online* helped promote the concept of small teaching to a wider audience.

I had always believed that the learning principles I had researched for both of those books were ones that applied to adult learners, college-aged students, and high school students. I wasn't quite sure about their applicability to elementary students, although my wife, a kindergarten teacher, had assured me that she saw them at play in her kindergarten classroom as I saw them in my college-level courses. But it was not until Sarah Connell Sanders had drafted the book that you hold in your hands that I became fully convinced that the concept of small teaching belonged in the elementary classroom as well. Sarah has translated the core ideas from the original book into a program that can improve the learning and development of your students through simple, everyday changes to your teaching practice.

I will confess, though, that what makes me especially excited to introduce this book to the world, and what makes it stand out in a crowded field of education books, is the quality of the writing. Although I earned all of my degrees in English literature, for the past two decades I have been researching and writing about education. I have learned from painful experience that many of the articles and books I read in this field are written with barely serviceable prose, designed to make a point and move on. But as someone who has continued to write about and teach writing and literature, I have a deep appreciation for a book that not only gives me great ideas, but presents those ideas in beautiful prose and engaging stories.

You are holding just such a book in your hands. I first became acquainted with the writing of Sarah Connell Sanders by admiring her essays in our local city magazine, where she writes about culture, food, fashion, and more. When I finally met her in person, and discovered that she was a veteran teacher and school librarian working in the same public school district where my wife also taught, I realized immediately that she was the ideal person to share the gospel of small teaching to elementary educators everywhere. As with *Small Teaching Online*, I made a small contribution to the creation of this book, but most of the words you will read are Sarah's. I hope that you will find as much pleasure as I have in reading her graceful prose.

One of Sarah's accomplishments in this book is the way in which it pushes the ideas from the original book into new territories, and offers new reflections on the idea of small teaching. You will find my favorite example of such a reflection in the book's introduction, in a pair of sentences that I wish I had written myself:

> I want to know the fundamentals of how children learn and then be allowed to use my own creativity and experience to apply those lessons to my own classroom. No matter what new state mandate or administrative fiat has been sent down to shape my classroom, I want to make sure I am still staying true to the basic principles of education that will ensure my students are safe, happy, and learning.

This might be the best description of what I hope all three *Small Teaching* books offer to teachers everywhere: an accessible introduction to some new research on how their students learn, some examples of how teachers can translate that research into daily classrooms routines, and a deep respect for the creativity and commitment of readers.

I have spent my whole life among teachers: my mother, my wife, some of my siblings and their spouses, friends from high school and college, and all of the colleagues that both my wife and I have worked with over the past two or three decades. Teachers have always been the most creative people I have known in my life. The teachers I know don't need to have someone standing over them and ensuring that they are doing their best work. They are dedicated to their work and to their students. Give them the information they need, and they will find ways to surprise themselves and their students with what they dream up.

I hope that Sarah's ideas, and the concept of small teaching, will give you some new fodder for your teacherly creativity. I hope that the opportunity to exercise your pedagogical imagination in new ways will inspire you to take renewed joy in your work. I hope, finally, it will give you a reminder of what inspired you to become a teacher in the first place.

James M. Lang, PhD
Worcester, MA
April 24, 2022

Introduction

Sarah Connell Sanders

s a teacher, I do everything in sixes. Six guiding questions. Six project deadlines. Six classroom stations. You get the idea.

Numerologists believe the number six is both stable and karmic. Mathematicians call six the smallest perfect number. Guitarists play with six strings. Bees build their hives with six sides. Gamblers risk their fortunes on the fate of a six-faced die. Coffins rest six feet under the ground.

I was not surprised to read the Pew Research Center's finding that one in six U.S. teachers work second jobs, making us three times as likely as U.S. workers overall to hold down multiple gigs, according to the U.S. Bureau of Labor Statistics (2019). In my years as a teacher, I have supplemented my own meager salary by waitressing, lifeguarding, coaching, and writing. I am the one in six, and I am tired.

So is Anne Lang, a 25-year veteran of public school teaching. Anne's husband, Jim, is the author of the original *Small Teaching*—a text geared toward new college professors. Anne and I are both educators, but we face a different crop of eager learners than Jim. I have spent the majority of my 13-year career corralling middle schoolers, and she has spent 25 years teaching the lower elementary grades, primarily kindergarten. We both find plenty of ideas and strategies that resonate with us in the original book because the learning principles identified by Jim are ones that apply to learners of every age. But college teachers have an enviable amount of freedom in terms of what they do in the classroom. Teachers at the elementary and secondary levels face a distinctive challenge, in that they have to learn how to balance what they know is best for their students with the demands of a number of other audiences: parents, politicians, and administrators. Negotiating the needs of all of these constituencies can create a climate in which teachers feel like they are being micromanaged from every angle.

"When August 1st comes around, I feel a sense of anticipation and dread," Anne confided in me. "Don't get me wrong, I always look forward to arranging my classroom, meeting my new students, and labeling materials with their names. I even welcome the initial staff meeting where we get to hear who got married, who had their first grandkid, and whose children headed off to college for the first time." But over the course of her first day back at school, at some point, Anne feels her new-school-year enthusiasm begin to dim when she hears the inevitable announcement of a fresh rollout, ambitious initiative, or program—effective immediately.

"Two years ago, we adopted a new math program," she said. "I work in a large urban district and we had already adopted a new program two years prior. I remember sitting in a hot overcrowded classroom with everyone, while the book company's facilitator reviewed a million slides of all the 'wonderful' and 'engaging' lessons and activities we suddenly had on our plate. They handed us student workbooks, teacher's editions, and new online login information for my kindergartners. My head actually began spinning."

I can sympathize. It happens every year. I have this moment where I think, "Is it too late to quit?" Federal data shows that about 8% of teachers leave the profession annually. A survey conducted by the RAND research organization found that after the 2020–2021 school year, one in four teachers considered quitting (Steiner and Woo, 2021). We stay because we love our kids and we want to make a difference. But, it can be hard to remember that when Chad from Unicorn Math Company is delivering a three-hour presentation in a stifling mop closet that you just found out has been converted into your new classroom due to overcrowding. Then the wi-fi goes down.

In Anne's case, she avoided teaching the latest new math program for as long as she could. Can you blame her? She was training up to 28 five-year-olds on routines, procedures, and expectations. It didn't help that she had no access to a laptop or a projector. Like so many of us, she went home each day feeling frustrated and disappointed with herself.

Her saving grace came in the form of Greg Tang, an elementary math guru who has authored a number of math picture books and created online math games and puzzles for young learners. Early that school year, Greg conducted a one-day workshop with Anne and her colleagues, but something felt different. He gave them the space to express their true feelings about the new math program. She realized she wasn't alone; everyone was intimidated. "It turned out, the program just wasn't working for so many of us," she said.

Greg encouraged the teachers to start thinking small. "He gave us tips on how to incorporate math throughout the school day," Anne recalled. The moment her head finally stopped spinning came when Greg gave her a piece of paper to fold. "If a kid can fold this paper into two equal halves, they are already on the way to mastering a first-grade math standard," he told Anne. It was a tiny tip, but she felt her confidence grow. "I realized that making small, but effective, changes in my math lessons would be the key to success for both my students and myself," she said.

Anne's experience of being asked to use some wholesale new teaching approach is not a unique one; I've encountered it as well. Sometimes I feel like public school districts have a big target on their backs to attract the sales staff of new programs, technologies, and software. Do I want my students to have access to the latest and greatest research-based best practices in education? Yes,

yes, yes! Do I want to miss class time for days or weeks of training on expensive new materials? No, no, no.

Jim and Anne have discussed this lower-ed problem at their dinner table more times than they can count. On one occasion when they were kind enough to entertain me, Jim pointed out, "The fact that such initiatives wash up on shore so regularly, only to be replaced by the next big wave of new ideas a few years later, has left so many educators across America skeptical of any outside efforts to shape the work they do for their students."

"And they're right to feel that skepticism," Anne interjected.

Jim continued, "Whatever wholesale program your school or district has decided to impose upon you and your fellow teachers this year, you know full well that it won't change the most fundamental challenge you face as a teacher: spending each and every school day engaged in the slow, hard work of helping your students learn."

"Don't get me wrong," he added, "large-scale educational initiatives can, at times, provide a useful framework for the daily work of teaching, but they can also get in the way of tried-and-true techniques that have always worked for you and your students. Worse, they can close your mind to the prospect that new ideas or research in education *do* have the capacity to help you evolve and grow as a teacher, and to improve the learning and achievements of your students."

And so Jim and I, armed with the insights of teachers like Anne and others you will meet in this book, began the work of applying the theory of small teaching, initially developed for college faculty, to the K–8 environment. What you'll find here is exactly what college faculty found in the original book and what online instructors at every level found in the first sequel, *Small Teaching Online* (a book that appeared, providentially, just before the pandemic hit): a sensible and manageable approach to enhancing the everyday work you do in the classroom. The small teaching approach is unique in the way that it identifies a small number of learning principles that are applicable to all students and then translates those principles into quick and easy teaching strategies for any classroom. Whether you are looking to enhance your existing practice or struggling to adapt to a new context or district-wide initiative, small teaching will ensure that the work of learning in your classroom will continue and improve.

Although this book might have special appeal to new and early-career teachers, I really wrote it for the weary, the disheartened, and the exasperated. I am already too old and exhausted to be sold an entirely new approach to education every year. I want to know the fundamentals of how children learn and then be allowed to use my own creativity and experience to apply those lessons to my own classroom. No matter what new state mandate or administrative fiat has been sent down to shape my classroom, I want to make sure I am still staying true to the basic principles of education that will ensure my students are safe, happy, and learning.

In this book, you will find exactly the tools you need to accomplish this objective. Together with Jim, I have highlighted a small number of principles identified by cognitive scientists as fundamental to the learning process. I have then outlined easy and concrete strategies for putting the principles into practice in your classroom. You do not need special materials or pricey technologies. I don't want you to radically re-think your hard-earned experience. My hope is for you to recognize these principles in the work you are already doing and make small modifications to enhance them further in order to have a substantial impact on your students.

I am a Massachusetts public school teacher and many of the individuals consulted for this book are also Massachusetts educators. As such, I have tried to represent a diverse range of voices across K–8 education knowing that Massachusetts consistently ranks at the top of the Quality Counts Annual Report Card, a comprehensive assessment of the nation's K–12 system by state. In 2019, Massachusetts ranked second to New Jersey after leading the Quality Counts rankings for four consecutive years. High standards and strong accountability practices aside, the Massachusetts teachers I spoke with were just as tired, fed up, and overwhelmed as everyone else. My hope is to compile the individual models, backed by research, that are helping to keep them afloat—all in one place.

The original edition of *Small Teaching* became so popular among college professors because it amounted to bite-sized steps that could be experimented with throughout the semester. The vast majority of my recommendations intend to do the same. Our models require little preparation and minimal (if any) grading. As Jim tells his readers, "If you have even five minutes of your day available to help your students succeed, then you are ready for small teaching." If his sentiment provides you with a glimmer of hope, you are not a part of the 8% (and counting) who will leave K–12 education this year. Small teaching is here to rejuvenate you.

Knowing: The Six-Minute Fix

S arah here—in Part I, I introduce basic learning princi-ples to help students master the basics of your lessons: facts, information, simple concepts and ideas, even basic skills—six minutes at a time. We begin with the lowest level of Bloom's Taxonomy: retrieving. It turns out that giving students multiple opportunities to retrieve information from their memo-ries is the most effective way for them to master basic knowledge. Similarly, the act of predicting encourages students to draw on their prior knowledge and strengthen their web of context for new information. Sprinkle in regular opportunities for students to get vocal and self-explain what they've learned, and you can transform your classroom in six minutes a day with a relatively light lift.

You'll recall my love of the number six. For me, it all comes down to a 1956 publication by psychologist Benjamin Bloom titled *Taxonomy of Educational Objectives: The Classification of Educational Goals, Handbook I: Cognitive Domain*. If you've spent more than five (or six) minutes in the field of education, you are likely already familiar with Bloom's conceptual framework. There are six major categories: (1) Knowledge, (2) Comprehension, (3) Application, (4) Analysis, (5) Synthesis, and (6) Evaluation.

When I introduce Bloom's Taxonomy to my middle schoolers, I explain that the first level of thinking demands uniform answers. Base-level questions all have one correct response. "What is the capital of Massachusetts?" Boston. "What is the sum of two plus two?" Four. Meanwhile, higher tiers can yield any number of responses. "Imagine if the villain defeated the hero in the final chapter." Or "Create a script that brings to life the account of a primary source." In other words, Knowledge tasks require a "right" answer, free of debate, whereas Evaluation tasks merit infinite opinions.

In 2001, one of Bloom's former students, Lorin Anderson, revised the taxonomy to suit the modern age of learning. Don't worry, there are still six categories in Anderson's revamp. Today's version of the Taxonomy includes the categories: (1) Remember, (2) Understand, (3) Apply, (4) Analyze, (5) Evaluate, and (6) Create.

General education teachers, special education teachers, teachers of English language learners, and everyone else (present company most definitely included) have made the mistake at some point of thinking that the lowest levels of the taxonomy can be bypassed in favor of higher-order thinking. Why should we focus on the facts, which just require memorization? Let's get right to the fun and creative stuff. But the literature on learning tells us that a solid mastery of the facts is precisely what students need if they are going to learn to engage in activities like applying, analyzing, evaluating, and creating. One educational writer, Ian Leslie, refers to facts and information as the "hidden power" of our thinking: the more facts you have at your disposal, the more deeply you can think about them. If you skip the ABCs or the basic rules of grammar, you probably aren't going to cultivate the next great American novelist in your classroom.

In the age of Google, skipping the basics can be tempting to students and educators. A decade ago, I became the first English teacher in my district to pilot a one-to-one iPad initiative. I remember feeling defeated at the end of the year when I asked students to complete a survey about their experience. One eighth-grader wrote, "I like having my iPad in class because instead of asking the teacher questions, I can just Google the answers." I felt as if I had been replaced. I was no longer the keeper of knowledge; I had become an accessory. As is the case in many modern professions, I was learning to augment the work of a powerful machine.

I came to understand that with Google at their fingertips, my students could rise through the ranks of Bloom's Taxonomy more quickly. But, access to limitless information did not mean I could dismiss exercises in Bloom's Level 1: "Remembering" and Level 2: "Understanding," nor did it make them any less important. Far from it. My students still needed to put in the time and energy to master basic information if I wanted them to progress into deeper levels of learning.

Education scholar Mark Bauerlein warns against lowered's fervor to reach higher-order thinking skills, such as analysis and evaluation, right away. In his research, he observed many teachers obsessing over making students analyze text features rather than helping them comprehend content. "They regard the emphasis on knowledge at the elementary level as a soul-killing boot camp of memorizing facts" (Bauerlein, 2020). But without a core knowledge competency, Bauerlein argues, critical thinking becomes nearly impossible. Students begin to see the results of their Google searches in total isolation. Mastering knowledge opens pathways for the analysis and creative thinking that lives at the highest echelons of Bloom's Taxonomy. Without factual knowledge, reasoning and problem solving have nothing to cling to.

As a simple illustration of the correspondence between facts and thinking, consider the example of a jazz musician building a performance in real-time, improvising based on the decisions of the other players. We might think of a jazz musician, with precise pitch and natural rhythm, as someone who is an adept and creative thinker. But, if she were to listen back to her performances, she could likely pick out specific notes, melodic contrasts, and so on. More importantly, the musician's gradual mastery of her instrument over the course of years of study and practice, enables her to take what she encounters throughout the performance and imbue it with deep meaning by making connections to previous jazz performances and preparing her for critical thinking during her next song.

The same is true of our kids. If I ask my seventh-grade English class to conduct a critical analysis of a Langston Hughes poem, the students with a contextual understanding of the Harlem Renaissance will outperform those who have simply googled the poet's bio. We need to store facts in our memories if we want to climb the rungs of Bloom's Taxonomy. Skipping steps will eventually result in a grave tumble from Bloom's proverbial ladder.

In an age of limitless access to information, students often hold biases or misconceptions about the science of their own learning. Memorization does not come naturally to most young people. When tasked with studying for a vocabulary quiz, how do most students respond? They Google the definitions, then they make flashcards, and finally, they commit the words to memory a night ahead of their assessment. Students who study this way might perform well on an assessment, but it's unlikely they will commit the words to long-term memory for future application.

Understandably, most teachers prefer to devote their time and energy to the highest tiers of Bloom's Taxonomy—naturally, the higher levels are more stimulating for both teachers and students. Regardless, the Taxonomy will crumble beneath our students' feet if there is no foundation. Short and simple adjustments to practice can allow students to improve their own recall, making way for deeper engagement with the meaningful and complex learning tasks, which we fully consider in Parts II and III.

Chapter 1

Retrieving

Retrieval is the foremost foundational skill taking place in our classrooms. My favorite memory of the retrieval effect goes back to a waitressing job I held in grad school. In retrospect, I spent far more hours waitressing to pay for my M.Ed. than I did on the Boston College campus. To fund my education habit, I worked at a farm-to-table restaurant called Armsby Abbey in the 2010s. It was the height of a "slow food" boom, which refers to the made-to-order nature of a kitchen, but never the service. At Armsby Abbey, we were expected to memorize all of the farms and an exhaustive list of ingredients on an ever-changing menu. Our customers always had a lot of questions.

> "What animal did the Blue Ledge cheese come from?"
> "Goat."
> "What was the apple-fed cow's name?"
> "George."
> "How fresh are the strawberries?"
> "I picked them myself, this morning."

A shift at Armsby Abbey might sound like an episode of "Portlandia," but it was my reality for five years—and I loved it. My family rarely dined out at restaurants when I was growing up, with the exception of my birthday. At Armsby Abbey, my palate blossomed. I learned to love pastrami beef tongue, smoky blue cheese, gobs of bone marrow spread on toast, and pickled watermelon rinds. Every shift felt like my birthday, with new oddities to explore.

We were routinely tested by management on pickle lists, allergens, and farmers' names. Coming straight out of grad school, this level of study felt natural. The career servers teased me about my binder full of flashcards and T-charts, but I knew what worked for me. A lot of them could memorize the list of 22 rotating draughts, the soup du jour, and the specials with just one glance. I, on the other hand, would ask my colleagues to quiz me in the back while we polished silverware and brewed coffee. The owners even went so far as to leave certain information off the menu to encourage guests to engage in conversations with us about the food. By the end of my tenure, I had a personal story for every farm—an asset that Google could never provide to my customers.

It made sense why the lifers had such powerful memories; practice really does make perfect, or close to it. This learning phenomenon is called the *retrieval effect*. Put simply, if you hope to retrieve knowledge from your memory, you should practice retrieving knowledge from your memory. The more you practice, the more capable your memory becomes. Without the frequent assessments at Armsby Abbey, whether they came from guests or management, I would not have been forced to routinely draw the information from my memory. Had I simply read my responses to customer questions from a cheat sheet tucked into my notepad, I would have never had to activate my memory. This would be the student equivalent of studying by reading the textbook over and over again—a practice that cognitive psychologists deem one of the least effective modes of retaining information.

At the restaurant, even when I forgot the beekeeper's town of origin, or heaven forbid, the flavor profile of a foraged elderberry, I was forced to practice drawing the information from my memory by finding the answer to guests' questions. The same principle follows suit for K–8 students in the classroom. The more they practice remembering something, the more firmly that content becomes lodged in their brains for the long term.

Contrary to popular thought, the brain is not a muscle, but our long-term memories can be trained like a muscle with frequent and deliberate practice. Our long-term memories are capable of building stamina in the same way a marathoner gains endurance as she delves further and further into her training. Her very first 10-mile training run might feel brutal, but come race day, mile 10 will have her feeling light on her feet. Alternately, our *working* memories are limited. An adult's working memory generally hits capacity at four new pieces of information. The best teachers are able to help students move as much information as possible from their working memories to their long-term memories.

Another name for the retrieval effect is the testing effect. We normally think about testing as *measuring* student learning, but what we learn from the literature on retrieval practice is that it can actually be a potent tool to *promote* student learning. This is because tests force students to engage in memory practice. Rather than just viewing tests (and quizzes) as learning measurement exercises, researchers have pointed to them as highly effective learning tools. Frequent assessment breaks allow students an opportunity to transfer information from their working memories to their long-term memories.

I'll be honest, when I hear "the testing effect," it evokes a wave of foot-tapping anxiety from deep within me. (Quick, somebody hand me a paper bag to breathe into.) It makes me think of standardized tests I have taken, and the standardized tests my students have to take. But the testing effect doesn't really refer to these kinds of high-stakes, one-off exams; it refers instead to the practice of "testing" student memories in frequent, low-stakes ways throughout the school year. We can get the testing effect in everything from daily reading quizzes to oral exams, to gamified online assessments.

These kinds of low-stakes memory practice exercises, or retrieval practice exercises, can solidify the knowledge base around which students begin to build complex networks of information in their long-term memories. The research about testing that we will consider in the following section refers to learners who are recalling information, concepts, or skills from memory in regular, short bursts. Later, when I talk about testing, I won't be referring to high-stakes final exams or standardized state benchmarks—I'll be talking about the kinds of quick activities that can take place in six minutes or less. These retrieval practices will refer to small teaching activities that can be implemented with minimal grading and little planning.

WHAT'S THE THEORY?

Recall the introduction to this part in which Bloom's Taxonomy is discussed. Retrieval practice supports the mastery of material at the base level of the Taxonomy, but that material is no less important than any other echelon of learning. Through retrieval, we solidify in our minds the facts, concepts, information, and basic skills that enable us to do our deeper thinking. Retrieval provides the foundation required for creative application and innovation.

The introduction of the Common Core Standards in 2010 did not just alter the content deemed most significant for American public-school students. The Common Core Standards aimed for the application of content across disciplines through writing and speaking in order to show a deep understanding of the material. This shift fed a public misconception that we had done away with memorization in schools—the biggest scandal since teachers stopped teaching cursive. In reality, the memorization of foundational information became more important than ever before.

Shortly after the rollout of the Common Core Standards, Arizona State University Researchers Peter Rillero and Helen Padgett acknowledged that education was moving away from rote memorization in favor of deep conceptual learning (2012). Still, Rillero and Padgett championed a key finding: "The role of prior knowledge is important to deep conceptual learning, as it may support or hinder learning new material" (2012). The prior knowledge they refer to here is what we can support through retrieval practice. When students are encountering new ideas, or facing new challenges in their learning, they will be best equipped to meet those challenges when they have a solid foundation of facts, information, and basic skills in their brains—and not just in their Google search histories. The stronger their long-term memories become, the more capable their working memories are of processing and holding new information.

The Memory Lab of Henry L. Roediger at Washington University in St. Louis has dedicated its work to test-enhanced learning and the belief that retrieval practice enhances long-term retention. But once again remember here that "test-enhanced" learning does not necessarily refer to those fingernail-gnawing experiences that we might associate with the word *testing*. In fact, the findings of the Memory Lab have been used by many teachers to identify small ways in which they can incorporate retrieval practice into their classrooms on an easy, everyday basis.

Three strategies that help students do this were discussed in a paper published by Roediger in 2018 in collaboration with Psychology Professor James S. McDonnell and Washington University doctoral student Oyku Uner. The first strategy, pausing to formulate a summary of a textbook chapter after reading, proved far more effective than merely rereading the chapter. But note that these summaries have to be conducted from memory, and not just from looking at the material again. Summaries like these are sometimes called brain dumps or free recall exercises;

students read the text, close the book, and then write a short summary of what they remember. Simple, fast, easy—and effective.

Next, Roediger and his colleagues suggested spacing out retrieval practice. "The longer the spacing, the greater is learning for the long term" (Roediger et. al., 2018). In other words, it's much better to engage in retrieval in three six-minute activities throughout the week than it is to engage in one 18-minute session on Friday. The more we space out our retrieval practice into different sessions, with time elapsed between them, the more effective that retrieval practice will be. For example, you might ask your students to retrieve something a few times during the first week of exposure to help them transfer the information from their working memories to their long-term memories. Then, you'll still want them to come back to the information a few additional times in the coming weeks and months to ensure it has been adequately lodged in the long-term memory.

Finally, Roediger and his colleagues recommend interleaving or layering the study of related topics, rather than engaging in the massed repetition of a single topic (2018). As *New Today* contributor Mary Ellen Flannery puts it, "If you were coaching a new basketball team, would you ever have a single 45-minute practice on a Monday and then expect your rookies to win a game the following Friday?" (2021). Of course not. Likewise, educators should not teach a new skill one week, then follow up with a test the following week and expect positive results. For example, if I were to teach my students the basic skill of writing a thesis statement, I might introduce the main strategies and have students practice retrieval through some low-stakes quizzing. Good start. But over the course of the year, as I am introducing new writing strategies, I should continually return to the skill of composing a thesis, and each time I do, I would ask them to remember the basic skills they have learned. Returning to thesis-writing time and time again in new contexts will be more effective than asking students to write seventeen thesis statements, one after the other, during the first month of the school year.

Another example of applying interleaving strategies was described by cognitive scientist Pooja Agarwal and Chicago middle-school math teacher Anne Agostinelli. They analyzed interleaving in the mathematics classroom because they took issue with textbooks introducing large blocks of problem sets focused solely on new skills. In these cases, they witnessed students "plug and chug"—falling into repetitive and predictable routines that did not require deep processing (Agarwal and Agostinelli, 2020). With interleaving, students were asked to tackle a range of problems, leading to far greater long-term retention of concepts.

Agostinelli grew especially fond of applying interleaving to her middle schoolers' homework assignments. Each week, she assigned five problems for homework, two of which referred directly to her current instruction and three that referred back to earlier content. Agostinelli praised the ease of interleaving, "It took remarkably little effort on my or their part," she concluded. "By organizing information in more meaningful ways, and applying powerful tools that are supported by cognitive science research, we can lessen the pressure and strengthen the confidence, joy, and performance in our classrooms" (Agarwal and Agostinelli, 2020). Not only did interleaving improve retrieval, it made her curriculum planning and preparation more efficient.

The means by which new information is introduced can also impact retrieval. Daniel Schwartz, Catherine Chase, Marily Oppezzo, and Doris Chin of Stanford University examined a common instructional sequence in K–8 classrooms intended to help students retain new information (2011). They found most teachers begin new units of study by telling students about a principle or skill and then assigning a series of directly related questions or problems. Schwartz, Chase, Oppezzo, and Chin sought alternatives through an experience-first approach. "The mechanics of these alternatives withhold didactic teaching at first," they explained, "lest it undermine the processes of discovery" (2011).

While initial test performance was the same for eighth-grade students regardless of telling-first or experience-first approaches, long-term transfer proved far more common among the experience-first group. The researchers found that telling-first caused students to zero in on one problem at a time, while experience-first caused them to seek out similarities and make their own connections—a surefire path to long-term memory (2011).

You might wonder whether all of these retrieval activities, even if they are very low-stakes, would just make your students anxious all the time. You might therefore be as surprised as I was to learn that giving your students frequent opportunities to engage in retrieval can actually *lower* their anxiety about testing. Henry Roediger was part of the first team to examine the relationship between retrieval practice and classroom test anxiety. In a survey of 1,408 middle and high school students, the study found, "For classes in which retrieval practice occurred, 92% of students reported that retrieval practice helped them learn and 72% reported that retrieval practice made them less nervous for unit tests and exams" (Agarwal et al., 2014). Despite researchers' suspicions that students would prefer to limit the number of tests taken in schools, results showed that more regular retrieval practice actually *decreased* their testing anxiety.

Retrieval comes down to familiarity and consistent practice. Whether you are taking orders in a restaurant or studying for a final exam, retrieval practice will help the long-term memories of your students to strengthen and improve over time, preventing the need to "cram" for exams. "When it comes to the trade-off of time versus content," say Agarwal and Roediger, "think about it this way: If students remember more, you save time by reteaching less" (2018). Your first and quickest entry point into the practice of small teaching, then, is to find as many ways as possible to inject into your classroom small opportunities for your students to stop, think, and draw from their memories whatever you want them to learn most deeply.

IN SHORT

- The levels of Bloom's Taxonomy are not a hierarchy; they are building blocks. Without achieving one level of thinking, it is nearly impossible to arrive at the next.
- The Common Core Standards are skills focused, but that does not mean content knowledge is irrelevant. The more prior knowledge of content a learner possesses, the easier it becomes to apply a new skill within that content area.
- Summarizing new information is a more powerful path to the long-term memory than rereading the new information.
- Spacing out retrieval practice is more effective for moving new information to the long-term memory than engaging in one long retrieval practice session before an exam.
- Refer back to information introduced earlier in the year on a regular basis. Do not compartmentalize units of study.
- Students who grapple with new information or a new skill prior to direct instruction will have an easier time transferring it to their long-term memory than students who receive direct-instruction first.
- Retrieval practice through frequent quizzing and testing actually makes students less anxious, rather than more so, for high-stakes assessments.

MODELS

The biggest barrier standing in the way of retrieval is time. Let retrieval become a consistent part of your routine by devoting just six minutes per day. The following models allow you to incorporate retrieval in bite-sized moments during both synchronous and asynchronous instruction.

Three-Two-One

One of the most common forms of retrieval I see in elementary classrooms is the three-two-one, a strategy first introduced to me by *Facing History*. Students are required to recall three facts from the previous day's lesson or homework, two things they want to know more about, and one lingering question. That's it. Couldn't be simpler, and couldn't be a more direct application of the theory of retrieval practice in the classroom.

Asking students to complete a low-level remembering task like the three-two-one will not only ensure that students are completing their asynchronous work, it will also lay the groundwork for a later higher-level discussion. Students should not be expected to recite minute details of a 50-page reading verbatim. Exercises in retrieval at the start of class, like the three-two-one, should instead focus on the most significant or primary elements of the required content. Retrieval practice will help students recognize the difference between their working memories ("I knew this yesterday, but I can't seem to remember it today") and their long-term memories ("I have a solid understanding of this and I can connect new information to it"). Rest assured, working memories grow stronger with age.

Bell-ringers and do nows are a nice opportunity to use strategies like three-two-one questions because every student is required to create hard evidence of their learning; whereas, if you just throw out the question orally and ask for volunteers, only a handful of students might actually get to engage in retrieval practice. Habitual participants are sure to raise their hands and provide their responses aloud, but quieter students will be robbed of the benefits of retrieving. Whenever possible, ask students to respond to activities like the three-two-one in writing or by talking to one another in pairs or small groups before you ask students to raise their hands and volunteer. Make sure every student gets the benefit of this powerful technique.

THREE things you remember
from yesterday.

TWO questions you still have.

ONE thing you enjoyed from
yesterday and want to know
more about.

Closing Questions

Like a bell-ringer at the start of class, an exit ticket at the end of class creates an opportunity to emphasize key takeaways from the lesson. Psychologists call this the "serial positioning effect," which says people generally remember the first and last things they hear or read (Flannery, 2021). The easiest closing question you can ask is also the simplest: What's the most important thing you learned today? But there are endless variations on this simple query: What did you learn today that you want to remember for the rest of your life? What did you learn today that you are still a little uncertain about? What did you learn today that made you curious about something? All of these questions require students to remember something from class that day, and thus give them a quick shot of retrieval practice.

You might even consider asking the same question at the start of class for your bell-ringer and at the end of class for your exit ticket. Sometimes an exit ticket can function as an opportunity to revise the written response created during the bell-ringer.

For example, if my lesson objective states, "Students will be able to recall three key details from the novel that contribute to the protagonist's characterization," then I might begin class by asking students to provide three adjectives to describe the protagonist based on the previous day's reading. For the exit ticket, I would expand on the opening question by asking students to provide a passage that demonstrates one of the adjectives they chose and explain why it correlates.

Processing opening questions together comes much more naturally than processing closing questions because of the standard timing of a class period. The bell-ringer can be addressed and discussed in various ways over the duration of the class, while the exit ticket is apt to linger as students barrel out the door. The longer misconceptions hang in the air, the more onerous they become. The last line of defense should be opening the next day's lesson with a clear explanation of the previous day's exit ticket. A better solution is to reveal the correct answer in the final moments of class or in a flipped classroom video students can watch at home as part of their homework.

One-to-one computing environments make it difficult for students to resist simply searching the internet for the answers when it comes to basic retrieval questions. Often, I ask students to answer on paper with their devices in "courtesy mode," meaning their Chromebooks are partially closed or their iPads are face down. Retrieval questions are not intended to be a scavenger hunt; they aim to improve memory function. Nearly every experiment and study I have read on learning and memory has featured a control group in which students are free to review their notes or textbooks. Time and time again, this method proves less effective than retrieval practice for the long-term retention of core information.

Bell-ringers and exit tickets should not feel like nasty surprises to your students. You can explain to them why these retrieval tactics are brief, but important parts of your daily routine. Logging off their computers and shutting their books will help them remember what they have learned, benefiting them in the long run, and laying the context to amass and apply more knowledge.

Big Basket Quizzes

Prepare for a BBQ. I'm not talking about burgers and dogs. In their book *Powerful Teaching*, Pooja K. Agarwal and Patrice M. Bain introduce Big Basket Quizzes or BBQs (2019). In this model, teachers keep a basket full of quiz questions at the front of the room and continuously contribute questions to the basket throughout the year. A few questions are selected at random for every quiz to help students retrieve foundational knowledge from earlier in the course.

The BBQ does not have to consist solely of questions from the basket. Instead, focus on recent and relevant content and then pull a few questions from the basket as supplements to provide retrieval practice. It's okay to put questions back in the basket for repetitive use. The more a question is drawn from the basket, the easier it will be for students to retrieve information they learned weeks or even months previously.

The basket can also come in handy if you find yourself with spare moments at the end of the day or the period. Ask for a volunteer to fish a question out of the basket and provide an incentive to students who answer correctly. You can even turn it into a competition. Divide the class into two teams and keep track of the score whenever someone answers a BBQ question. Get into the practice of pulling a BBQ question every day during morning meeting and then again during dismissal.

Multi-Part Quizzes

Consider quizzing in two parts. Begin by posing assessment questions for students to complete individually. Then, ask students to tackle the next set of questions in small groups. The second stage of quizzing could include the most complex question from stage one, or you could try posing an open-ended question to help facilitate collaboration. Either way, students will benefit from providing or receiving peer feedback.

You can get a little creative with this one. For example, Kansas psychology teacher Jen Schlicht is in the habit of creating retrieval grids, which she likens to a bingo card. "You put questions of varying difficulty on the grid and assign point values to each question," explains Schlicht. "A question on today's content might be worth 1 point. Something from last week might be 3. Something harder might be 5" (Flannery, 2021.) Students are given a set amount of time to earn as many points as they can independently or in groups. Not only does the grid help students to retrieve old material, it also provides the perfect structure for a multi-part quiz. Ask students to complete as much of the grid as they can independently and then pair up with students who can help them fill in their gaps.

By instituting multiple parts for each quiz, students will be able to tackle more complex concepts. The stages of quizzing should follow one after the other in a single class period. Group dynamics can be troublesome for certain students, especially those who are motivated by achieving high grades. Use your judgment to decide how much you weigh each part of the quiz. I prefer to reward successful group responses, but never penalize unsuccessful groups. In other words, the group's work can only improve but never detract from an individual grade.

Adding a collaborative part to your quiz will also help to alleviate grading by consolidating the number of responses to which you have to provide feedback. Allow students to discuss, explain, and retrieve among themselves. Do your best to make the groups equitable. To ensure fairness, avoid grouping together those who finish the independent part first. Pre-determine your groups with inclusion in mind.

Polling

Rather than calling on individual students and asking them to retrieve information in front of the class, polling encourages full class participation without risk of public humiliation. During virtual schooling, I found myself utilizing the polling feature of Google Meets nearly every day. Polls, or audience response systems, are quick and easy ways to take the pulse of a class and encourage retrieval practice in a low-stakes environment. Google Forms offers equally compelling and instantaneous data that can be displayed to the whole class. The teacher can see how individual students respond, while the full class data remains anonymous. Implementing a screen of anonymity will help students to overcome their anxieties and actively participate in class.

Polling is a great way to practice retrieval. Build up a database of questions to recycle throughout the year. You don't have to feel confined to multiple choice questions when it comes to polling. Platforms like Socrative, Poll Everywhere, Kahoot, and Pear Deck allow you to ask open-ended questions and display significant answers for class discussion.

You can also use polling to cultivate student ownership. Allow students to contribute to your database of questions throughout the year. A 2020 study psychology professor Mirjam Ebersbach and her colleagues at the University of Kassel found that students who generated their own quiz questions performed a full letter grade higher than students who simply revisited the material. Your learners will be excited when they see their question get pushed out to the whole class. Better yet, you won't have to spend hours formulating all of the questions for retrieval practice by yourself.

PRINCIPLES

Building a base of foundational content material is pivotal for students in the earliest years of their education. Start by incorporating regular opportunities for retrieval with the simplest material on your syllabus. The following principles intend to guide you through the models of small teaching retrieval, but they can be easily tailored to your own grade level or discipline.

Frequency Matters

The more students practice retrieval, the better they learn. Consistent quizzing is not old-fashioned; it should be your default. Quiz your students for six minutes every class period, with or without grades, if it fits into your routine. Online tools like Gimkit, Google Forms, and Socrative can dramatically reduce grading, but not every assessment needs to be graded. Formative assessment is the most valuable tool in your toolkit for gauging the effectiveness of your own instruction. Formative assessments should be reviewed to clear up misconceptions, but they should not contribute to a student's final number or letter grade on a report card. Use bell-ringers, do nows, and exit tickets as a means for frequent quizzing. Whatever strategy, or mix of strategies, you choose, implement them with consistency.

Align Practice and Assessment

The questions you intend to ask on your summative assessments (midterms or final exams) should resemble the questions you have used for retrieval practice throughout the year. If you ask students to memorize all of the colors of the rainbow in Spanish, make sure to refer to those color names as much as possible throughout the year in other contexts. If you use multiple-choice questions on your summative assessments, incorporate them in day-to-day activities as games or low-stakes competitions. If you plan to use open response questions requiring the synthesis of retrieval and critical thinking, assign writing exercises in class that do the same.

Require Thinking

Give your students something to think about. Retrieval practice can be as simple as a basic memorization exercise; every third grader needs to know their multiplication tables. But, rather than asking students to commit a chart of numbers to memory, I might start with a word problem. "I want to provide a bottle of water for every member of our class after recess. If there are 20 members of our class, how many will I need? How many bottles will I need for the whole week?" By creating an authentic context for a brief retrieval task, students will be more likely to engage and master the material.

SMALL TEACHING QUICK TIPS: RETRIEVING

Memory retrieval exercises are brief. You can carve out a moment or two in every class period, but the most effective use of your time will likely come at the opening or closing of class. Regular quizzes or writing prompts are my preferred form of retrieval practice.

- Use bell-ringers and do nows as an opportunity to ask students to recall information from the previous class session. Try the three-two-one approach. Ask them to recall three key details, two lingering questions, and one thing they want to know more about.
- Use exit tickets at the end of class to ask students to write down the most important takeaway of the day.

- Compile key questions throughout the school year for "Big Basket Quizzes." Draw old questions from the basket at random throughout the year to supplement regular assessments.
- Use polling platforms to pose questions for the class in a low-stakes environment. Continue adding questions after each unit until you have a rich database that is representative of your full course.

CONCLUSION

In my first year of teaching, I decided it was important to let my students take some ownership over the curriculum. Students would preview the following week's text every Friday and select three potential words for our weekly vocabulary list. They'd write their choices on a sticky note, sometimes campaigning with their seatmates to choose the same terms. When the bell rang, they'd smack their sticky notes onto our classroom door and head off for the weekend.

I still remember the delight of one struggling reader named Catherine who arrived at our classroom on Monday morning to find her word, *loquacious*, on the official vocabulary list. It became an inside joke between the two of us. She'd be chatting off-topic during class months later and I'd give her my teacher-stare.

"Sorry Miss," she'd say, "I'm just feeling loquacious today." I couldn't help smiling.

Last week, I ran into Catherine at a Red Sox game. She is 25 now, and a far cry from the pre-teen who sat in my classroom so many years ago. Without skipping a beat, she walked over to me and said, "Miss, do you remember me? I'm your most loquacious student!" How could I forget?

I have met many teachers who take great pride in never "teaching to the test." I made similar remarks at the start of my career. I wanted my students to get lost in the magic of literature and debate. Why taint their youthful curiosity with constant quizzing?

Flash forward to dozens upon dozens of class discussions with students who had not actually done the reading, but were very skilled at faking their way through, and then retained none of the salient information by the end of the school year. No matter how many cute projects or lively class periods resulted, I came to understand that if I had not contributed to the long-term memories of my students, then I had failed them.

On days when I lose sight of the lasting impact educators can have, I like to return to the words of one of my mentors, Superintendent Erin Nosek:

> I think working in education is the best job you can have, and I mean that sincerely. Every day, we get the opportunity—whether it's as a classroom teacher, a paraprofessional, a cafeteria worker, or a superintendent—to impact the lives of children. That is a very special calling and a unique opportunity. Our collective responsibility in education is to support the development of children so they can maximize their potential and pursue their dreams. We need students to have access to the content and resources that are important to them. We need students to build a foundation so that when they graduate, they are ready for whatever they choose to pursue. We also need our students to feel physically, socially, and emotionally safe, and to ensure that they have whatever support they may need. We are trying to educate the child from a very young age all the way up to high school with the goal of everyone graduating and receiving all that they need in order to maximize their potential. I'd argue that it's the most important job you can have. It's really special.

I understand looming fears that you might be compromising your educational philosophy in some way by incorporating routine retrieval. The truth is, retrieval practice will help students master the foundational knowledge they require to revel in the wonders of your content area and engage in deep, intellectually charged discussions. It takes no more than six minutes a day. Your students will be grateful for the consistency and accountability. Be transparent. Tell them what you expect them to know. If our tests are based on the learning standards, there's certainly no shame in teaching "to" them.

Chapter 2

Self-Explaining

One summer, my principal called to offer me "an exciting opportunity," which in my experience, translates to him running through the halls yelling, "Help! I am so desperate and I will not take no for an answer." I was granted a handsome stipend in exchange for sacrificing my prep period to teach a sixth class. "You are going to love these kids," he promised. "They are your kind of crew." I had no idea what that meant.

On the first day of class, I found myself accompanied by 13 boys and 2 girls, all of whom had been assigned a second English class due to their less than stellar scores on the state exam. We met during the period when their peers enjoyed a second elective class like theater, art, or physical education. They were not pleased. Among the members of my "bonus" class, I had a third of the basketball team, the gregarious class president, and a notoriously gifted shoplifter.

The principal was right, these were "my kind" of kids. Most of all, they were vocal. Not a wilting blossom in the bunch. In addition to perpetual chattiness, we all shared another weakness, the dreaded reader fog. Like them, as a pre-teen, I had suffered from the torture of decoding an entire dense page of my independent reading book, only to realize I had been wondering when the cute boy who sat in front of me during math class would finally ask me out. Thinking aloud helped to clear the fog, although I always got some grief from teachers for being too social. It came as no surprise that my "bonus" class also took to thinking aloud right away.

"Really?" they asked when I introduced my reader fog remedy. "We can just yell out whatever pops into our heads while we're reading?"

"Well, you don't have to yell," I said.

We began reading *Where the Red Fern Grows* by Wilson Rawls. They made an insufferable chorus.

"Miss, can you bring us on a hunting field trip?"

"Did you guys know I was a dog in a past life?"

"Do redbone coonhounds actually have red bones?"

"Who would win in a fight, a mountain lion or Darth Vader?"

"Carissa stole my pencil case when I was in the bathroom!"

Carissa, whose name is not actually Carissa, also stole my phone at some point during the year. She would have made a talented cat burglar, but I think the experience may have actually reformed her. The more we became comfortable with the sound of our own voices in class, the easier it was to delve deep. When she returned the phone, of her own volition, it came with a sincere apology that taught us both a lesson about redemption and self-explaining.

Throughout class, I tried to clarify that thinking aloud was more than just piping up with free associations. "We're trying to make predictions and form connections based on our prior knowledge," I told them. They improved with time, and I watched them grow more and more invested in the story itself. By the tragic end, no one could contain their tears. Even the toughest among us (Carissa, obviously) was touched by the loyalty and love exemplified on the page. The basketball players cried like precious little babes.

Self-explanation is one of the most powerful tools in our arsenal for deep learning; I've seen it work time and time again. In my experience, we spend too much time quieting down children in our classrooms. It turns out an extensive body of research tells us that inviting learners to speak aloud their thought process while they are learning something new can support deeper learning. The researchers call this self-explanation. In other words, learners benefit greatly from explaining aloud what they are doing during the completion of a task.

As I recall, my noisy "bonus" class showed 12% higher growth on the state test that year than the grade level average because self-explaining helped them engage in active reading and encouraged them to build connections. Even the most reluctant readers can often be duped into talking about themselves and how their life relates to a book. Self-explanation opens the stage for personal connections, debate, and skill-based practice. Start with just six minutes a day. The best self-explanation not only prompts learners to explain what they are doing, but also *why* they are doing it. Tying the doing to the knowing is the shortest path to growing.

WHAT'S THE THEORY?

Little kids are honest (sometimes too honest). If you get a bad haircut or spill a cup of coffee in your lap on the ride to school, avoid the kindergarten wing. They rarely mean to insult; it's just a matter of lacking the self-regulation necessary to keep quiet. I'll bet at some point in your youth you were given the sage advice, "If you don't have anything nice to say, don't say it at all." While I wholeheartedly agree with this sentiment, I think we should be cautious when telling our children to pipe down.

Sit in the next room from any small child playing by herself and I guarantee you'll hear her think aloud. "I'm making you a cup of tea now, Betty," my niece will tell her favorite doll. "I know you had a hard day at school and this will make you feel better; we just need to wait for the water to boil and then we can add the tea bag." I'm sure she is simply mimicking the words of her own mother, but I relish the chance to hear what goes on inside her little head. "Be careful Betty! It's hot," she warns.

In my niece's game of tea party, I recognize her understanding of sequence, safety, and social-emotional well-being. It would be a shame to tell her to stop talking to herself. Creative chatter is nothing to be embarrassed about. Youngsters reach their imaginative peak while they are at their least self-conscious. For this reason, we should be encouraging kids to talk to themselves and explain their decisions aloud as frequently as possible. Maybe this looks like my niece's game of tea party or maybe it looks like a middle schooler live streaming a video game while he talks his followers through every move. Whatever it may be, self-explanation will help learners recognize problems or gaps in their own understanding and empower them to begin filling those gaps—or provide you with the opportunity to fill them.

For example, in one study of 205 middle school students, researchers found instructional explanations and self-explanation prompts, along with worked examples, positively impacted learning outcomes (Huang and Reiser, 2012). Worked examples refer to model responses that include the step-by-step process to arrive at a solution. Imagine looking at someone else's scratch paper from a math test while you try to solve a series of similar problems. When paired with self-explanation, worked examples can help students make enormous gains.

Sample Question	Worked Example and Self-Explanation
$6 + \_\_ = 10$	*I drew a picture using symbols to figure out the missing number from the equation.* $******+ \heartsuit\heartsuit\heartsuit\heartsuit = *******\heartsuit\heartsuit\heartsuit\heartsuit$ $6 + 4 = 10$
Lupita had 5 diamonds. She gave 3 to Troy. How many did she have left?	*I drew a picture using symbols to visualize the number of diamonds remaining.* $\diamond\diamond\diamond\diamond\diamond$ Lupita's Diamonds $\diamond\diamond\diamond$ Diamonds for Troy $\diamond\diamond$ Diamonds Remaining

Now, you try! Solve the problem below. Show and explain your work.

$13 - \_\_ = 9$

In the study, five mini-lessons were administered to seventh and eighth graders regarding proper comma use. The first half of each lesson, across all conditions, included examples of correct comma application. The second half of the lesson also provided certain groups with self-explanation prompts, instructional explanations, or a combination of self-explanation prompts and instructional explanations (Huang and Reiser, 2012). The achievement was then measured based on an assessment of 18 sentences without any commas. Students given both self-explanation prompts and the worked examples showed the strongest learning outcomes and spent the most time on task (Huang and Reiser, 2012). It follows that the more we prompt our learners to talk themselves through challenging tasks, the better off they'll be.

One teacher who uses the power of self-explanation regularly is Jennessa Burks, a fourth-grade teacher in the Cambridge Public School system, a city probably best known for America's oldest and most prestigious university, Harvard. Burks is a huge proponent of using first drafts and scratch paper to help model self-explanation for her students. "We provide students with worked examples frequently," she told me. "And when I say frequently, I mean there's a push for us to do it daily. I think students often learn well from each other by sharing their individual thought processes as they solve a new problem or approach a new task." For instance, Burks often models the editing process for the whole class using a checklist before having students engage in the process in pairs. Her worked example remains available for students to refer to throughout the lesson. "This helps them prepare to conduct writing conferences themselves," she said. "I often think it's helpful for students to get a bigger picture by looking at a worked example before they dive into an assignment, especially when it comes to something that might take some more abstract thinking or feel like a larger project to tackle" (2021). Burks never assumes her fourth graders have the innate ability to explain their thinking. She shows them what it looks like, provides them with a checklist, and pairs them strategically until they are comfortable thinking aloud on their own.

Thinking aloud is a form of metacognition. Metacognition, the understanding and awareness of one's own thought process, can begin very early in a child's development. For example, in Ontario, Canada, a play-based full-day kindergarten curriculum was first introduced in 2016 and has warranted great success (Braund and Timmons, 2021). The Ontario model asks kindergarten students to narrate their own thought processes in three distinct ways: metacognitive knowledge, metacognitive experiences, and metacognitive regulation. Metacognitive knowledge requires recognition of strengths and weaknesses. For example, a kindergartener might say, "I am very good at sharing my toys, but it's hard for me to remember to say please when I ask someone else to share their toys." Metacognitive experiences require articulating one's own problem-solving processes and strategies. For example, "I know what sounds the individual letters make, so when I put them all together, I can sound out the whole word." Metacognitive regulation requires setting goals and asking clarifying questions. For example, "I want to be able to write my full name by the end of the year. What is the best way to practice?" The Ontario curriculum urges educators to model the use of problem-solving language in support of these three forms of metacognition.

Teaching children to think aloud before they become too self-conscious about it gives us an opportunity to peek inside their minds and clear up lingering misconceptions. Researchers Heather Braund and Kristy Timmons pay particular attention to the role that co-regulation plays in Ontario's kindergartens (2021). The Ontario curriculum describes *co-regulation* as a means for innovative thinking when learners are: "collaborating with peers to create and modify things, using their own ideas, and building on the ideas of others" (Braund and Timmons, 2021). In addition to a learner dictating his thoughts aloud for his own benefit, Braund and Timmons emphasize the ways in which peers and teachers can also benefit and support one another through co-regulation. Engaging in metacognition, or thinking aloud, in front of others is a pivotal element of the Ontario program's success.

In their research, Braund and Timmons conclude, "It is imperative that co-regulation becomes a hallmark of Kindergarten programming. Given the important role that co-regulation can play in the early years, policymakers need to provide explicit (and theory-based) definitions of co-regulation and social shared regulation" (2021). One concrete example of co-regulation in the Ontario curriculum allows students to design their own play environments and negotiate their own selection of materials. Obviously, this level of student voice requires tremendous resources. The models that follow attempt to facilitate metacognition and co-regulation without breaking the bank or maximizing an entire lesson. Self-explanation can, in fact, be succinct, painless, and priceless.

Psychologist Tania Lombrozo of Princeton University recognizes self-explaining as a way of achieving the sensation of the "aha" moment:

> There's a phenomenon called the self-explanation effect that I think most people have probably experienced. And that's the experience of coming to understand something better as a result of trying to explain it to yourself or to somebody else. Part of what's sort of mysterious and amazing about the phenomenon is that that's a kind of learning that occurs even though you're not getting new information from anybody else or from the external world. You're just rearranging and scrutinizing what's already in your head. And in the course of doing that, you can sometimes have one of these "aha" moments and come to realize that you understand something better, or sometimes come to realize that you thought you understood something but there's actually an important gap in your knowledge that you need to fill. (Vedantam, 2021a)

As Lombrozo points out, self-explanation is not just about discovering truths, but also recognizing falsities. By encouraging students to speak their understandings aloud, they are likely to experience either an emotional rush of satisfaction or the motivational pull of dissatisfaction. The stronger the sensation, the more defined their neural pathways will become. You know what that means—a long-term memory is imminent.

IN SHORT

· Providing learners with worked examples (a more experienced learner's draft or scratch paper that "shows their work") will help novice students talk themselves through new types of problems and skills.

· Encourage students to verbalize their strengths and weaknesses during play and collaborative work.

· Praise students for explaining their problem-solving strategies to their peers and give them ample opportunities to do so.

· Model goal setting at the start of every lesson by sharing your learning objective aloud and urge students to do the same by articulating their own goals on a regular basis.

· Start as soon as possible. Children can become self-conscious about self-explaining if the behavior is not normalized among peers early on.

· Students who can self-explain are able to rearrange the information in their brains to arrive at an "aha" moment.

MODELS

Self-explanation is a pivotal path to improving learning outcomes. Don't fret about the noise. By implementing these simple small-teaching techniques, you can get into a productive routine and cut out the chaos of everybody speaking at once. Make time for students to turn-and-talk. Take intentional breaks and prompt students to identify the underlying principles, themes, and main ideas emphasized in your lesson. Students don't need to generate these principles for themselves—consider providing a list of possibilities, then asking students to choose and defend just one. Over time, they may become capable of articulating underlying principles in their own words, but particularly in the case of new material, this added step can often place too many demands on the working memory. Start small. Find an exciting stopping point and model what self-explanation looks like for your students.

Think Aloud

The gold standard for self-explanation is thinking aloud. Students who learn to think aloud are more likely to receive peer insight while also scrutinizing their own thought processes in a constructive way. It can be awkward to talk to yourself, particularly for self-conscious or shy students. To ease the pressure, I create privacy walls by cutting tri-fold project boards in half or propping up large three-ring binders on students' desks. I have even employed small sections of PVC pipe to give students the sensation of talking on the phone while they think aloud.

In her 2018 column for *Literacy Today*, researcher Molly Ness describes the benefits of modeling the think-aloud process for struggling readers. "Think-aloud is helpful for a wide variety of readers across a wide variety of text; benefits have been documented for struggling readers and English learners and with different genres, content areas, and formats," Ness writes. "Moreover, students enjoy think-aloud, which serves as an energized, brief instructional burst that helps young readers to take on the strategies modeled" (2018). Ness suggests locating "juicy" stopping points in advance of think-aloud lessons, urging teachers to resist asking simple comprehension questions in favor of modeling their own independent reading practices for their students.

In order to help students pause and articulate what they have read or observed, I provide sentence starters like the following:

> When I read this page, I picture . . .
> I can tell that . . . because the story says . . .
> I think this chapter is mainly about . . .
> One thing I can do to try to solve this problem is . . .
> This reminds me of . . .

The more students practice thinking aloud, the less nerve-wracking it becomes. Sometimes teachers, especially online, feel as if they are only providing value through direct instruction. Don't fall into the scholar-academic trap. Your knowledge cannot trickle down to your students' brains through osmosis. Encourage them to speak up as frequently as possible. Self-explaining isn't always quiet or tidy, but it makes a profound impact on learning.

How Does This Connect to Our Goal?

Learning objectives, also known as learning goals, should not be kept secret. I explicitly tell my students that if at any point during class, they find themselves staring out the window and thinking, 'What's the point of this, anyways?' They should look at the objective on the board to find the answer. I will often prompt these sorts of self-explanations if I see a student struggling with independent work. Kneeling down next to their desk, I point to the objective and say, "How does what you're doing right now connect to our goal for the day?" I find this form of gentle redirection very helpful.

Self-explanation can improve a wide variety of learning outcomes across disciplines, ranging from STEM projects to long essays or oral presentations. If a student is assembling a slide show or a final paper, it is not necessary to redirect them to the objective for every single paragraph or every single slide. Instead, try asking them to choose one paragraph or one slide and explain the choices they have made. Ask probing questions:

> "What strategy for creating an effective presentation did you use?"
> "How did you organize this particular slide?"
> "How does your essay connect to our year-long theme?"
> "How does your project connect to one of this week's goals?"

Hopefully, students who are able to articulate their choices and strategies for one chunk of the assignment will be able to apply the same logic across the entire finished project.

Susan Ahrendt (Metropolitan State University), Debra Monson (University of St. Thomas), and Kathleen Cramer (the Rational Number Project) test drove this practice with fourth-grade math classes for a 2021 article in *Mathematics Teacher: Learning and Teaching PK–12*. The researchers encouraged practitioners to anticipate student thinking, circulate, and monitor student responses before carefully sequencing the students who would share out for the whole class to hear. Teachers who were strategic about scaffolding responses and beginning with common errors, found it easier to motivate participation and guide discussion to eventually arrive at the correct conclusion. Students provided with the space to share their "meaty" thinking with classmates were more perseverant, analytical, and willing to take risks (Ahrendt, Monson, and Cramer, 2021).

Turn-and-Talk

Cognitive scientist, Laurie R. Santos teaches the most popular class in Yale University History, "Psychology and the Good Life." She is also the host of a popular podcast called "The Happiness Lab." In her research, Santos has studied how social connections increase our happiness.

"Social connections are a critical component of feeling happy," Santos told me. "Even a brief interaction with a stranger can boost our mood, and being around other people also seems to be associated with feeling happier. By making more authentic social connections in the classroom, we can be sure to improve student mental health" (2021) As a result, all of my students are assigned a turn-and-talk partner for brief breaks throughout class during which time I ask them to share their ideas or contemplate problems.

The turn-and-talk, as a form of peer instruction, was made famous by Harvard physicist Eric Mazur who would ask a question for students to work out independently and then share with a neighbor to help guide revisions. Mazur used "clickers," a form of personal response technology that allows students to submit their answers for immediate review. For a tech-free option, I like to use whiteboards, asking students to hold up their answers so only I can see and then share their board with a turn-and-talk partner to make changes as necessary. If most of my students answer the turn-and-talk question correctly after sharing it with their partners, I move forward to the next agenda item. If not, I pause to reteach or clear up misconceptions for the class.

Turn-and-talks may not come naturally to students at the start of the year. Feel free to provide lists of prompts, sentence starters, and underlying principles to help guide their brief discussions. Sometimes asking students to generate their own principles can exhaust or distract them. Writing a list of main ideas to choose from on the board is especially helpful if a student has elected to change her answer after consulting with a peer. I will often ask, "Which idea or principle on the board led you to your first answer, and which one now seems correct to you?" The self-explanation that follows will illuminate gaps or misconceptions and help guide my next steps of instruction.

Turn-and-talks do not have to be limited to two students at a time. In fact, a team of U.K. researchers recently examined 71 studies in which students were asked to discuss or collaborate and found that students of all ages learned more when they discussed or collaborated in groups of two, three, or four—outcomes were even stronger when students interacted one-on-one with an adult (Barshay, 2020). Obviously, you won't be able to work one-on-one with every student every day, but you can get in the habit of regularly inserting yourself in turn-and talk groups throughout class. During turn-and-talks, I also try to keep an eye out for students dominating the conversation to remind them to share the floor with quieter students.

Discussion Protocols

Plenty of the adults I work with are not particularly skilled when it comes to sharing airtime during conversations, so expecting discussion skills to come naturally to my students is unreasonable. Setting rules and time limits for speaking can help ensure everyone's voice is heard. Sometimes I even assign specific roles during discussions to make sure one student is asking follow-up questions, one is looking for real-world connections, one is defining unfamiliar vocabulary terms, and so on.

Above all else, discussion protocols emphasize respect. The National School Reform Faculty (NSRF) is my go-to resource for teaching kids to talk to each other and to themselves. Its website offers more than 200 protocols designed for efficient use of class discussion time. As I mentioned, a lot of grownups don't understand how to share their airtime or ask follow-up questions, so it seems unrealistic to think these skills will come instinctively to children. By establishing hard and fast rules for discussion, each protocol has a gamified feel to it that students come to enjoy.

Before I share some of my favorite NSRF protocols, I want to warn you that the first go-around of a new discussion protocol can be disastrous. Just like any game, the rules take getting used to. If a protocol results in pandemonium the first time, consider trying it again the next day. As students become more accustomed to the rigid guidelines for discussion, they will come to value a sense of order and routine. At the end of each protocol, there is time for reflection. Don't skip this step. Ask students what they liked about the protocol and what proved challenging. You may find the reflection period to be the most powerful opportunity for your students to practice self-explanation.

One protocol I use regularly with great success is called "The Final Word." Students sit in groups of four and independently brainstorm the solution to a problem in silence. A timekeeper is then identified to help facilitate their discussion. The first speaker is given a specified period to share his or her idea—usually, one minute provides plenty of time. If they run out of things to say during that minute, the group can silently contemplate what they have shared so far, but they may not respond until the minute is up. The three other group members are then allotted 30 seconds to speak. They may pose questions, offer constructive criticism, or build on the first speaker's idea, but the first speaker cannot respond until every group member has offered their feedback. The first speaker is then given the final word with one more minute to respond while their group listens. Each group member has the opportunity to act as the first speaker and give the final word before the protocol comes to an end. The whole protocol takes only a couple of minutes per group member, but every voice is heard.

Another NSRF protocol I use frequently is called "Text Rendering." For this activity, students are asked to pick the "most significant" sentence from a reading. The whole class stands in a tight circle and each student takes a turn reading their sentence aloud with no explanation. If someone speaks out of turn or says anything other than their sentence, we start over. Next, the process is repeated for the *phrase* they find "most significant" in the reading. In the third and final round, students share a *single word* they find "most significant" from the reading. Then, we open the circle up for discussion. I ask guiding questions such as, "What words or phrases did you hear repeated most frequently?" and "What common themes emerged as we went around the circle?" It's not often that you get to hear every student's voice during a single class period; I love Text Rendering for this reason.

The final NSRF protocol I use on a consistent basis is called "Three Levels of Text." For this structured discussion, students are asked to analyze a passage in three different ways. Level one is "on the line," meaning a literal interpretation. Level two is "between the lines," meaning a symbolic interpretation. Level three is "beyond the lines," meaning a thematic interpretation that relates to the larger text or the real world. Each student is given up to three minutes to describe their passage on all three levels and then the group is given a total of up to two minutes to respond.

One of my veteran colleagues, Mary O'Donnell, has led the Debate Club at our school for many years. She keeps it simple. "We organize students into two groups," she explained. "One group will argue the 'Affirmative' point and the other group will argue the 'Negative' point. We give the students a statement. The 'Affirmative' side must come up with arguments that claim the statement is true. The 'Negative' must come up with arguments that claim the statement is not true" (2021). O'Donnell allows each side just 10 minutes to formulate a strategy. "One person on the 'Affirmative' side gives their argument first, then the 'Negative' side counters with their first argument. The debate continues in this manner until all arguments have been heard, ending with the 'Negative' side." Students are provided an additional 10 minutes to devise their rebuttals to the arguments they have heard. As students become more adept at the format, O'Donnell limits the teams to three speakers each.

O'Donnell does not shy away from hot button issues. Students debate topics such as gun violence, politics, and school policy. Anne Vilen and Ron Berger of *Educational Leadership* suggest establishing "guard rails" for discussions of especially divisive or controversial subjects (2020). Vilen and Berger recommend the 4 A's protocol, requiring students to record an assumption, an agreement, an argument, and a question to ask (2020). Ensuring a sense of security by employing protocols like the 4 A's will help your students to find their voices.

PRINCIPLES

Self-explanation is perhaps the most basic small teaching technique in this book, but it does not come naturally to most students. Model for them. Prompt them. Pair them. There are plenty of people in front of whom I would feel embarrassed if they caught me singing in the shower or talking to myself while I cooked dinner. There are also people who I wouldn't think twice about catching me in solo conversation. Be the latter. Make your classroom a safe and comfortable place to get caught talking to yourself. Embrace the noise.

Scaffold Self-Explanation

The most difficult part about self-explanation is learning to do two things at once. Initially, you might want to offer sentence starters or a list of underlying principles to get them talking. As they become more skilled at generating these things for themselves and more comfortable with the sound of their own voices, you can provide them with more freedom.

Point to Principles

Self-explanation helps students to connect theory to practice, principles to concrete steps, and knowing to doing. Even if you choose to provide a list of theories or principles for students tochoose from, they will ultimately need to form a meaningful connection for themselves. Try to create opportunities for self-explanation that require them to articulate a selection and describe how it connects to the task at hand. As they search for solutions and make revisions, encourage them to find the words to explain why.

Utilize Peer Power

I find self-explanation can be tricky in classes that are too small or too large. If there are too few participants, talking to yourself can feel daunting. If there are too many, your voice gets lost in the crowd. Ideally, a pair of students can act as one another's audience so the self-explanation feels as if it has been directed at a companion. Self-explaining is most useful when it elicits feedback, so don't be afraid to jump in or bring everyone back together for an opportunity to share with the large group.

SMALL TEACHING QUICK TIPS: SELF-EXPLAINING

Self-explanations can take place during any sort of cognitive task to increase mindful learning. Remember to identify stopping points throughout your lesson for self-explanation to take place. Make students feel comfortable hearing the sound of their own voices.

- Push students to think aloud and tie their knowledge of information, principles, theories, and formulae to the specific task they are completing. Encourage them to articulate how what they know is connected to what they are doing.
- Assign every student a turn-and-talk partner. After they arrive at a solution independently, ask them to turn and discuss it with their partner, and then revise their own answers accordingly.

- Ask students to choose an underlying principle or the main idea from a list on the board and explain how it connects to the task they are completing. Then, encourage them to explain how the task connects to the daily objective.
- Use strict discussion protocols with clear rules to provide structured opportunities for self-explanation. Always leave time for reflection to debrief after using a discussion protocol with students.

CONCLUSION

I have never turned in a piece of writing to an editor without reading it aloud to myself. Something about hearing my own words pass through my lips helps me to recognize the errors I am blind to on the page. I pause and say, "Well, that doesn't make any sense." Then, I devise an edit. I am no longer ashamed when strangers catch me reading aloud in an empty room. Many of the smartest people I know talk to themselves. The benefits we receive from this practice are ones that our students will experience as well. Normalizing structured self-explanation in my classroom has helped students recognize their own errors—and correct them—in an impactful way. I model thinking aloud, daily.

One of the greatest benefits of self-explaining is that it fosters active engagement during class time. Think of self-explanation as an especially helpful strategy for your students in the early stages of mastering a new cognitive skill. Practicing metacognition will help students solve math problems, write papers, and conduct science experiments with a purposeful and mindful approach. In addition, self-explanation allows ample opportunity for teachers and peers to correct misconceptions before they linger.

Go ahead, turn up the volume.

Chapter 3

Predicting

My best friend and I host a pop culture podcast together. Awards season is always an exciting time for our show, as it allows us to make predictions about who will take home the top prizes. We make a point of trying to see as many Academy Awards nominees as possible before the big event.

We often lament the fact that many of the organizations charged with bestowing entertainment awards have historically favored white men, including the Academy of Motion Picture Arts and Sciences. Keeping this in mind, we frequently discuss on our show who *will* win versus who *should* win. We find that sharing our picks publicly on the podcast and airing our personal opinions adds some emotional investment before the broadcast takes place.

There have been many upsets in Oscar history, but who could forget the controversial 2017 mix-up of *La La Land* and *Moonlight*? The crowd watched in disbelief as presenter Faye Dunaway misspoke and announced *La La Land* as the Best Picture and then moments later corrected her error to proclaim that *Moonlight* was the true victor.

On the podcast, I had predicted that *La La Land*, a musical about old Hollywood starring two white Hollywood A-listers, would take home the Oscar based on the bias of the Academy. Nevertheless, I had argued that *Moonlight*, which features an all-black cast and explores queer themes, was the more deserving film of the two. In a way, both of my predictions came to fruition when *Moonlight* defied the odds. The reason this mix-up is such a memorable moment in Oscar history for me is because I remember being rocked one way and then another. As I watched the drama unfold, I felt like I had a stake in the game because I had made a prediction that *Moonlight* should win but assumed it would likely be snubbed. I was intellectually and emotionally invested, and those investments lodged the results more firmly in my memory.

The experience of predicting the outcomes of awards shows reflects a basic principle that cognitive researchers have emphasized for decades. Making predictions about material you hope to master will increase your ability to remember and understand it. One of the reasons that happens is because making a prediction activates your current knowledge about a subject, warming up your brain and preparing it to learn new information in the subject area. Successfully selecting the outcome of an entertainment award show requires knowing or remembering a bit about each of the nominees. How many awards have they won or lost in the past? Did they win or lose based on the historical bias of the voting body? Did they perform better or worse than expected? Acknowledging the obvious fact that answering these questions will not guarantee a perfect prediction record, the more I can recall about each nominee, the more informed I will be in predicting a categorical winner.

Making predictions also stirs up emotions that can help motivate and drive learning. Watching a series of Academy Award nominated films feeds my curiosity about who will take home the prize. I am thereby less likely to check social media or fold laundry while I watch a nominated film, and instead pay close attention. I also feel pleasure in making correct predictions, even when they do not correspond with my own personal preferences. Emotions have the power to focus our attention and provide cognitive fuel. My emotional attachment to making a prediction about Best

Actor or Best Director helps it to secure a place in my long-term memory.

The power of prediction extends far beyond my enthusiastic ruminations on a pop culture podcast. Predicting offers a direct route to help our students acquire knowledge and comprehension without great fanfare or time commitment. In this chapter, we view predicting as a natural and advantageous inclination in the *Small Teaching* classroom that takes nothing but six minutes or less out of your day.

WHAT'S THE THEORY?

Testing out our abilities before we are ready is a form of prediction, but sometimes it can be a dangerous one. Last summer, I decided to take up skateboarding. I watched a series of YouTube videos and even a MasterClass by skate legend Tony Hawk. I hopped on my board with great confidence, cruising the neighborhood until I came to a steep downhill and promptly broke my arm. Learning by listening, reading, and watching a pro skateboarder, prior to getting on the board was only so helpful. At a certain point, I had to get on the board and try it for myself. I found that Hawk's instruction was well and good but unresponsive to my individual needs. I had failed to master how to slow down or stop. It wasn't until I took a serious fall that I discovered what I needed. When my arm healed, I sought a skilled local skateboarder for hands-on instruction. That was the point at which my real learning began. I don't recommend breaking your arm as any form of pretest, but I can say my initial failure left me eager to learn from an experienced instructor and fill in my knowledge gaps.

As teachers, we facilitate this type of learning in our classrooms every day, asking students to try out cognitive skills they have yet to master. I don't spend the whole year lecturing about active reading practices and then test them on *Moby Dick* come June. I assign short readings from the start of the semester, even though some of the skills they need won't be covered until midway through the school year. Furthermore, I pair students strategically and encourage them to gather context from one another.

Prediction supports learning in three distinct ways. First, prediction improves retention and comprehension of learned material. Consider the best practices of modeling and simulation that are emphasized in the Next Generation Science Standards (NGSS), a set of research-based, up-to-date K–12 science standards introduced by the National Research Council in 2013. The NGSS standards encourage students to formulate scientific questions and make predictions before planning and carrying out investigations. The standards rely on a cyclical design process, which naturally encourages students to make predictions.

During my four-year stint as a fourth-grade STEM teacher, I put the NGSS standards to the test in the wake of Hurricane Harvey. I tasked students with researching residential architecture and designing a hurricane-proof house. They were given a budget and the cost of materials. (A paper towel tube was priced at $400, a square foot of aluminum foil at $2,000, etc.) Each group built its model to scale with the understanding that it would have to withstand 30 seconds of wind from a leaf blower and the torrential downpour of a gallon of water.

On hurricane simulation day, we made predictions about which designs would weather the storm free of damage and why. Students cheered and jeered as they watched the other groups attentively in order to take note of their strongest features. After the first simulation, I asked the groups to go back and make alterations. "Redesign your failures," I told them. Nearly every group was able to apply what it had learned from its predictions in the first trial in order to improve the stability of its own house model for a second trial.

Predictions are not limited to the science classroom; they can be found across the curriculum in K–8 education, particularly when it comes to literacy. The second distinct way in which prediction supports learning is by forcing students to make personal connections and form attachments to their own approaches or theories.

A 2020 study of fourth-grade reading instruction demonstrated how prediction improved student learning in literacy instruction. Students who engaged in literature circles showed huge gains, as opposed to students in text-centered classrooms (Birsen and Kaya-Tosun, 2020). In the study, literature circles provided a collaborative approach to reading comprehension and elevated student voices and personal experiences. By contrast, the text-centered approach fostered a more independent process limited to discussing content directly from the book.

Researchers found that literature circles encouraged students to work as a team, with each member taking on a designated role to propel active reading and discussion. Literature circle roles often include jobs like connector, questioner, and illustrator in order to weave a web of context around reading and practice higher-order thinking skills, including prediction. On the contrary, text-centered instruction in the study relied on retelling the story and identifying its main ideas. Text-centered responses thereby focused on the simple summarization of a book, whereas reader-centered responses moved beyond summarization in order to forge personal connections with the content of a book (Birsen and Kaya-Tosun, 2020).

Researchers saw a steady decrease in text-centered responses and a continuous increase in the reader-centered responses of literature circles. "In other words, it can be said that students develop a personal response to the book with the literature circles, make more connections with the events in the book and show a desire to participate in the story" (Birsen and Kaya-Tosun, 2020). Students who engaged in literature circles participated in active reading, analyzing passages for foreshadowing, making predictions, and assessing their correctness among peers. A student in a literature circle might even be asked to take on the explicit role of "predictor" and make a prediction about what would unfold in the next chapter. By making a public prediction, the stakes become more emotional and the readers become more engaged.

An important distinction between effective and ineffective predictive activities is that effective predicting warrants immediate feedback. Lingering misinformation sometimes leaves a deep impression; it seems likely that the sooner correct information arrives, the better—if not during the same class session as the prediction activity, then at least by the following class. The correction does not necessarily have to come from a teacher. At times, peer learning can be a more powerful method for encouraging students to take risks.

Finally, making predictions requires a fair amount of trust and willingness to fail. It takes a particular classroom culture for predictive activities to reap their full potential. This is the third distinct manner in which prediction supports deep learning.

Darcy Schwartz is an art educator for whom I have particular admiration in my home city of Worcester. She serves over 300 students per week at her community studio, which she designed to make art affordable and accessible for all local youth. Schwartz is very open minded when it comes to her teaching practice, but she has one steadfast rule: "We don't have erasers on our pencils here because I don't want anyone to feel like if you're just sketching something or drawing something that you need to erase it to make it perfect," she told me. "It is already perfect because if you just keep sketching, eventually it can become what you want it to be" (2019). Schwartz's attitude conveys confidence and assurance. The absence of erasers does not prevent her from helping students to hone their skills, it simply signals the value of problem solving and risk-taking in her studio.

Your students are capable of making predictions before they learn new material by following these basic models and the ones I introduce next, which will not cost you more than six minutes a day.

IN SHORT

· Ask students to make predictions before they carry out investigations and simulations of a problem.
· Assign students specific reading roles designed to strengthen emotional investment, including an official "predictor." By sharing predictions publicly, learners will develop a stake in the game.
· Provide immediate feedback. If a prediction contains illogical conclusions or blatant misinformation, don't let it linger.
· Foster an environment where learners feel safe to take risks. Stoke curiosity with frequent pauses to make predictions.
· Use predictive activities to inform heterogeneous groups of students. Strategically pair novices with experts.

MODELS

The ideal moment for predictive activities is at the beginning of a learning experience. The opening of class is a perfect chance for students to make predictions based on your learning objective and agenda. Bell-ringers and do nows have become commonplace over the last two decades, so much so that I think we sometimes forget the power they have to boost learning by way of prediction. Once in a while, I catch myself including bell-ringers and do nows in my lesson plans simply because they are requirements on the teacher evaluation rubric, without regarding their true value. Consider the following models for leveraging the opening of class, the opening of the semester, and the opening of the school year as opportunities to make predictions.

Predict during Do Nows

Bell-ringers and do nows are brief independent activities meant to increase time on learning by maximizing productivity at the start of class. Bell-ringers and do nows are also the perfect opportunity to ask students about previous lessons. Instead of providing an overview for your students, give them the context of the larger unit and ask students to answer the following questions:

- What was the goal of yesterday's class? How do you predict it will apply to the items you see on our class agenda today?
- Make a prediction about a character who will change or grow in today's reading.
- We have conducted several experiments on matter throughout this unit. Based on what you have learned, make a prediction whether the following objects will float or sink.

What does a bell-ringer or do now look like across disciplines? Here are a few things I have seen work first-hand that will require students to make predictions, and require you to do very little or no grading at all, and minimal prep.

English: Journals and quick-writes are the simplest way to activate prior knowledge and prompt predictions. Inspirational quotes and open-ended prompts about the day's lesson inspire creativity and individualism. I like to provide sentence frames or sentence starters to help hesitant writers get right to work. For example, students reflected on the following prompt before reading "The

Lady, or the Tiger?" by Frank R. Stockton in which a princess must choose the fate of her lover.

Example: Would you rather never see your best friend again OR see them enjoying themselves everyday with your worst enemy? How do you think this predicament will come into play in "The Lady, or the Tiger?"

Social Studies: Sequence scramblers are a great way to help students consider cause and effect while helping them make a prediction about a historic event. Provide three items from a timeline on the board without dates and ask students to put them in order.

Example: Unscramble the following events to place them in the correct sequence. (A) Travelers take covered wagons for westward expansion in search of gold and land. (B) German immigrants begin building covered wagons in Pennsylvania. (C) The prairie schooner is developed to travel farther distances.

Science: I've seen many science teachers utilize the Frayer Model in their classes to help students make predictions about the meaning of content vocabulary (Frayer and Klausmeier, 1969). Students can use a four-square graphic organizer to devise a definition, example, nonexample, and use the term in a sentence or sketch it out. Then, they research the true definition and make adjustments accordingly.

Example: Define *Adaptation*. Provide an example of an adaptation in the animal kingdom. Provide a nonexample of adaptation in human behavior. Draw a human or animal adaptation.

Definition:	Example:
A change or the process of change by which an organism or species becomes better suited to its environment.	A polar bear's fur is white for camouflage against the snow.

Nonexample:
Many people struggled to adapt to a new way of life during quarantine including social distancing and mask-wearing.

Illustration:

Term:

Definition:

Example:

Nonexample:

Illustration:

Math: Present students with two truths and a lie, then ask them to predict which equation is inaccurate and explain why they predict it won't add up.

   Example: (A) 6 – 5 = 1, (B) 5 + 1 = 6, (C) 5 – 6 = 1

One of my colleagues, Jeremiah Wright, uses do nows to help his students predict their social and emotional needs for the class period. Not only does this type of prediction help to inform his instruction, it also helps students take ownership over their own attitudes. "I like asking them to describe what mood they will be in by the end of class in three words or less," Wright told me. "They love this, and at the end of class, I save a couple of minutes to let them reflect" (2021). Wright's use of prediction to gauge social and emotional learning contributes to the sort of secure class-room culture that makes students willing to take risks and tackle new challenges.

Pretesting

Pretests come in all shapes and sizes. You can design a major pre-test at the start of the year that mirrors your final exam, a unit pretest at the start of a new course of study, or a brief six-minute pre-test to correlate with your class objective. For example, at the start of a unit on coding, I might ask students to define the following terms: *algorithm*, *loop*, and *bug*. Some students might think of the term *loop* as referring to a belt loop on their pants. I can use this prior knowledge to apply in the context of coding where looping means repeating a sequence more than once. Based on student responses, I tailor my instruction to their needs. At the end of the unit, I ask them to define the three terms again and have them compare their responses from the start of the unit to the end of the unit. Hopefully, they can now apply the terms appropriately within the context of coding.

Quick daily pretests are often the easiest type of pretest to incorporate into a regular routine. Consistency is key. Design your short pretests in the same format as your longer summative assessments. If you plan to use multiple choices in the mid-term, then use multiple choices on the pretest. If you plan to use an open response for the graded exam, then use an open response for the pretest.

Are you ready for the best news? Pretesting can help you to compact your curriculum. My colleague Craig Doyle begins every mathematics unit with a pretest to eliminate unnecessary ele-ments of his course load:

Pretesting gives me insight into what skills students have already mastered. When a majority of a class shows that they have already achieved mastery on a topic, it allows me to use the differentiation strategy of Compacting. Compacting is a technique that provides me with different options on how to move forward with a group. These include diving deeper within that topic, assigning a fun project to show mastery on that topic, or I can just move along to the next part of the curriculum while keeping that same fast pace. It also allows me to push individual students forward while I work on a smaller student group to reach mastery levels. Whichever way I decide to go, it keeps student engagement at a higher level when they are not bored with tedious, already familiar, class material. When we dive deeper they are challenged, and when we speed through a strong pretested topic to the next one, the pace is keeping them interested. Ultimately, this allows above average classes to move quicker through the curriculum, allowing more opportunity to dive deeper content wise or getting into the next year's topics when done with grade level curriculum (2021).

More good news: there's no need to waste time painstakingly grading pretests. That said, they should be collected and perused in order to gather a baseline understanding of the class' entry point. Provide immediate feedback by reviewing correct answers with the whole class and asking students to check their own work. In all cases of pretesting, especially with young children, you should make your intentions clear. Make sure they do not feel as if they are being unfairly assessed on material that has not been reviewed in class. Talk to them directly about the power of prediction and create a sense of transparency around your methods, especially for activities that might be misinterpreted as graded assignments.

Anticipation Guides

Anticipation guides ask students to express their opinions or ideas in the form of a survey response before approaching a new unit of study. They often provide broad generalizations about class material with which students are asked to agree or disagree. As class ensues, students are encouraged to reflect on why their predictions were accurate or inaccurate. For example, before reading the allegorical short story "The Lady, or the Tiger?" by Frank R. Stockton based on Ancient Rome, my middle schoolers answer a series of agree-or-disagree questions such as:

· I believe in fate.
· Destiny causes inevitable events in our lives.
· We all get what we deserve.
· It is okay to punish those who wrong us.
· I would rather never see my true love again than see them marry someone else.

Students' answers are displayed anonymously on a pie chart before we set to work reading. A debate follows, fueled by the data collected from our anticipation guide.

For students with preconceived notions about their own abilities in a certain subject area, anticipation guides are an excellent entry point because they rely on personal experience or opinion. In the case of "The Lady, or the Tiger?" students may not be familiar with the story's setting, based in Ancient Rome, but they can certainly make an evaluation of whether or not they believe in fate and destiny. As a result, reluctant readers are curious to see if the story will support their beliefs and therefore the experience makes them eager to keep reading.

In a history class introducing the civilization of Ancient Rome, the anticipation guide might include agree-or-disagree statements such as:

- Staying loyal to old friends is a moral responsibility.
- Your parents deserve respect no matter what.
- If you are asked to go to war for your country, you should say yes.
- Only men can recognize what is good and honorable.

Students will leave this exercise with a sense of inquisitiveness and a thirst for knowledge about Ancient Rome's social norms and unwritten laws.

Google Forms makes surveying students very simple. Google Forms also provides clear visualizations of the results with just one click. Responses can be viewed in anonymity, which is especially useful in certain contexts when students might feel insecure or vulnerable.

The reading specialist in my building, Deborah Donahue, frequently uses anticipation guides to hook her struggling readers. "I use anticipation guides with my students to develop their interest in the text; I find the results can turn into great conversation on meaningful topics," she told me. "After our discussion of the results, I ask them to use their prior knowledge to write predictions and I model the process to show them what the habits and behaviors of a good reader look like" (2021). Not only do Donahue's students become emotionally invested in their own predictions, they also become emotionally invested in her predictions—playfully gloating whenever they are right and she is wrong.

Tea Party

My favorite prediction protocol for any new unit of study comes from Kylene Beers in her book *When Kids Can't Read, What Teachers*

Can Do. "Tea Party offers a chance to consider active participation with the text and gives active adolescents a chance to get up and move around the classroom," explains Beers. "This pre-reading strategy allows students to predict what they think will happen in the text as they make inferences, see casual relationships, compare and contrast, practice sequencing, and draw on their prior experiences" (2003, p. 94). I have used Tea Party with students ranging from third through eighth grade with great success and never a dull moment.

For this activity, I scrawl significant words and quotes from a reading on individual slips of paper and mix them all up in a teapot. Students fish for a slip from the teapot and examine their selection. I set a timer for six minutes and ask students to mingle as if they are attending a real party. The goal is to take a look at everyone's slip of paper and begin to formulate inferences and predictions about the article or story we are going to read. When the timer sounds, students return to their desks and write a prediction using the sentence starter: "We think this reading will be about . . . because . . ." I seal the predictions in an envelope and return them to their owners at the end of the book to determine who came closest to the truth. In addition to drawing on prior knowledge, Tea Party forces students to consider causal relationships and practice sequencing. For example, before reading an article about Archimedes's law of buoyancy, I might prepare the following terms for my teapot:

- Pure
- Bathtub
- Overflow
- "Eureka!"
- King's Crown
- Is it gold or silver?
- ". . . filled a vessel to the brim with water"
- Physical volume

Students would compare their slips of paper and attempt to concoct an explanation for their connections to one another. Then, we would read the article about Archimedes together that tells the tale of Archimedes making an important scientific discovery from the comfort of his bathtub. Students who find they made the correct prediction will celebrate. Meanwhile, they are building a web of context in which to weave the truth.

Closing Predictions

Not all predictions have to be made at the beginning. Predictions can close class just as easily as they can open them. Often, closing predictions will apply to an asynchronous assignment completed at home. You may find an exit ticket requiring six minutes of effort provides a boost of interest and attention as students embark on an evening of homework. The responses can then be incorporated into the following day's bell-ringer or do now to analyze their own state of understanding and observe its evolution. For example, if you close class by asking how they think a novel will end and then return their responses at the start of the next class, they should be able to tell you what actually happened at the novel's conclusion and why they got it right or wrong. Try asking:

- At first I thought . . . but now I predict . . .
- I think that . . . will happen next because . . .
- I predict the main character will . . . because . . .
- I predict the solution will be . . . because . . .
- Considering the data showing . . . I predict that . . .

When you are forced to make a prediction without sufficient prior knowledge, you instinctively dig around in your mind for any possible information you have on the subject matter to help form a plausible prediction. When the answer is finally supplied, you have a secure space to process and store it in your memory because you have made the emotional investment necessary to do so.

PRINCIPLES

Making predictions requires little to no preparation, but leaves an enormous impact—an ideal activity for the *Small Teaching* classroom. The following principles can help guide you to create six-minute prediction activities for your classroom.

Stay Conceptual

Predictions elevate learning because they force students to gather prior knowledge in order to make an educated guess. If you ask very specific questions that negate the usefulness of any prior knowledge, you will see little benefit. For example, asking students to predict the outcome of a complex calculus equation will offer no value to a student learning his multiplication tables. Focus prediction activities on large concepts that have the potential to maximize later learning.

Provide Fast Feedback

Do not forget to close the loop as soon as possible. If your students make a prediction during the bell-ringer, address their answers before the end of class. Conversely, if predictions are made at the end of class, they should be addressed during the next day's opening activity. Make sure incorrect information does not hang around for too long. The briefer the life of a misconception, the better.

Leave Time for Reflection

Prediction is an accelerator of thought. Note the students who make correct predictions and lean on them as the "more knowledgeable others" to assist students who will benefit from a peer's assistance. Ask students: Why was your prediction right or wrong? What led to your prediction? What actually happened? Students who have made incorrect predictions should be encouraged to articulate the correct ideas in their own words.

SMALL TEACHING QUICK TIPS: PREDICTING

We have already discussed the merits of retrieval and memorization as a foundational practice. Meaningful prediction relies on the collection of prior knowledge and the ability to formulate complex connections. That doesn't mean negating quick strategies to incorporate prediction into your classroom. These reliable prediction activities will set you on the right track:

· Provide students with six minutes to make a prediction from the moment they walk through the door. The task should require no direct instruction for students to get started. That way, you can take attendance while setting a productive tone and activating prior knowledge and curiosity via prediction.
· Begin the course, unit, or class with a short pretest that correlates directly to your final assessment. You do not need to grade pretests. Use them as a sample set to help inform your instruction and condense your curriculum.
· Survey the class anonymously using an anticipation guide made up of simple agree-or-disagree statements. Share the results and correct misconceptions.
· Encourage students to make predictions together about a new unit of study based on a list of key terms.

· Pause before the conclusion of a problem, an experiment, or an entire lesson and ask students to make a prediction. Close class with an exit ticket asking students to predict what material will be covered the next day. Close the loop by correcting any misconceptions that arise.

CONCLUSION

In the opening of this chapter, I acknowledged my personal experience making public predictions about the Academy Awards on a pop culture podcast. I found the act of predicting drew me into films emotionally and urged me to pay closer attention. The mechanics of learning and prediction can likewise be considered from a cognitive perspective. Emotion and attention play a valuable role. Predictions tap into our egos, making us ask the question, "Will I be right?" Predictions also provoke curiosity, stimulating our brains to stay focused. Asking our students to make predictions is often the shortest path to curiosity.

Feeling compelled to inquire about a new topic is a pivotal step to maximizing learning outcomes. In fact, a 2019 Turkish study examined student questions as a means for increasing meaningful learning and motivation (Huner, 2021). In the study, Huner cites the positive correlation between curiosity and question asking. He draws on the observations of researcher A.R. Zolfagharia stating, "curiosity causes children to ask 125 questions daily while it triggers an average of 6 questions among adults with a logical worldview" (Huner, 2021). What better time to capitalize on prediction than when our students are young and curious? Consider how you can use the opening or closing moments of your class to prime your students to spin the silk and weave the web of deep and lasting learning in six minutes or less.

Chapter 4

Putting It All Together: Jennifer Hedrington, Grade 7 Teacher

I n 2021, Jennifer Hedrington was named the Massachusetts Teacher of the Year because of her profound dedication to the young people in her classroom. Hedrington worked in Baltimore and Houston before accepting her current position in the Malden Public Schools. I had the opportunity to speak with her on the importance of retrieval, self-explaining, and predicting in her middle school mathematics classroom. Where does she find the energy to be the best? Small teaching, of course.

How do you incorporate retrieval into your classroom routine?

I work with 13-year-olds. We do a lot of song and dance. I try to tap into whatever music is popular at the time and get them excited about math. For a lot of kids, math is not their favorite subject. Opportunities for repetition and practice are important. When you recall a concept over and over, it becomes like a song or a melody. I have kids who come back and tell me, "When I had to take freshman algebra, all my classmates were asking me what I was singing." It's a matter of catching their interest to help them remember. I teach math through stories. I've had kids who are now in college that say, "Whenever I have a test, I still remember the story you told us about integers."

I imagine turning a rule into a song gives them an easy context to help them remember it. Do you return to past songs throughout the year?

I use songs and stories to intertwine concepts we've learned in the past with what we are learning now. All of my word problems become relevant stories. I know a lot of textbooks chunk practice problems to focus on one skill at a time, so it's important to continuously ask students to go back to older material that is relevant to what we are learning now. We take breaks. I call them my commercial breaks. We pause and I tell stories to help the kids put it all together.

It's so easy to compartmentalize skills when you follow the textbook.

For the last 11 years, I actually haven't had a textbook. It allowed me the freedom to incorporate my own stories and word problems.

Were you able to find any credible resources online to lighten your load?

Prior to COVID, technology had not entered my classroom very much. A lot of my students were like, "Miss, for someone so young, you're so old." I'm old school in the sense that I'm comfortable with chalkboards and chalk. But with COVID, I was forced to embrace technology. For the first few months, I would cry every day after school. I'm not naturally tech savvy. For example, it was because of my students that I got a smartphone. I was happy with my flip phone and they were like, "Miss, you need a smartphone to keep up with us!" They teach me. During COVID, I learned how to make a Google Slides presentation for the first time. I began assigning choose your own adventure math homework. I would break up a slide into six boxes. And in each box, there would be six activities of different levels targeting the same skill. They ranged from really easy to medium and hard. I offered games like Jeopardy and Wheel of Fortune, but I also included a traditional worksheet option. Believe it or not, some kids still prefer traditional models. Of the six different formats, all they had to do was complete three of the six over the course of the week. On the slides, I also included videos of an individual teaching a lesson on the targeted skill. I understood that not everyone preferred or understood direct instruction from Ms. H. I encouraged my students to stop and say, "This isn't working. Let me see if I can learn it from someone else." So, I provided videos of other people teaching the same lesson with a slightly different approach. My students had a range of needs. They might say, "I really don't want to hear a male voice right now. I'd rather hear a female voice." There would be an option for that. To be honest, they might look at my version of the lesson and say, "I really don't want to hear this from you right now when I can hear it from a cartoon." It's the reality. Right? I would attach YouTube videos to the slides teaching the same concept with different approaches. If a student didn't come to school that day or wasn't paying attention because remote learning was so difficult—whatever the situation—the lesson was still available to them. This made planning much easier for me. I was like, Why didn't I do this for the last 17 years of my career?

I think it's important to find ways to help kids achieve mastery without burning out ourselves as teachers.

Yes. One thing I started doing was using online resources to help students raise their assessment grades. If I gave a quiz that had 10 problems and the kid got a 3 out of 10, which is a 30%, they would have an opportunity to raise that grade. I'm a big advocate of not giving children less than 50%. If the kid was like, "Miss, I wanna take it over again." I was like, I know my burnout threshold; I don't feel like giving another quiz because that means I have to grade another quiz and if 130 kids want to do it over again, that will become double the work for me. What I did instead was I started using a website with lessons to match each quiz. I told them, "You have 48 hours to get it done and whatever score you get, you bring it to me." As an educator, you get to see how long they spent working on the site. I would get the scores back and see this kid was on it for 3 hours, and 90 problems later, he had earned a 100%. I was like, "Who am I to take that away from the kid?" I put 100 in the grade book.

I agree with your policy. Failing students and immediately going forward with the curriculum seems like it prevents learners from moving much of anything into their long-term memories.

The traditional grading policy is not fair. If I were to tell you that you had a 60% chance of crashing during a flight, would you get on the plane? Most people would say no. If I told you you had a 60% chance of getting a divorce if you married this man or this woman, would you do it? No. But as children, when they walk into a classroom, they have a 60% chance of failing because the grading system goes from 0% to 100% and a failing grade is from 0% to 59%. That's 60 points of failure. I push my students not to let a teacher give a 30%. It doesn't make sense. It's not fair. Everything else is in increments of 10%, except for the letter *F* and the kids who are most harmed by that letter *F* are children of color, economically disadvantaged students, and students with special needs. They just reach a point of no return and believe it doesn't matter. I do professional development sessions with teachers where I talk about cheating. When a kid cheats, most educators say, "How dare you be so dishonest?" I say, "You're looking at it the wrong way; if a kid didn't care, they would not even write their name and turn in a piece of paper. When a child is cheating, they're telling you they care. They're crying for help. They're cheating to try to survive." We are all human. We all mess up.

How do you use self-explaining to elevate the student voices in your classroom?

I am huge on student voice. When I talk to my students, I remind them I'm not a teacher, I'm an educator. I tell them that I only teach math because I need health insurance. Right? I'm here to educate the entire child, the whole child. Honestly, my class is like 40% math, 60% the rest of the child. I advocate for kids to raise their voices in math and also in life. I tell them when I make a mistake or feel embarrassed. I apologize in public. I have to be the living example. I want them to know that it is okay to make a mistake and talk through it. It's known in my class that I welcome students to disagree with me as long as they are willing to speak on it. I'm not always right. If you can come up with a good argument proving I messed up, then I'll give you the credit. I'll fix it to benefit you. Normalizing these conversations helps students make progress in their own learning and in their school community.

How do you create an environment where students are willing to take risks, not just by raising their voices, but also by grappling with new problems and making predictions?

I tell my students, some of us are Chia Pets. They receive the information, get a little water, and boom! They've got it. But me, I'm a maple tree. It takes years for me to understand things. Especially with the pressures of COVID, I feel like we're expecting all of our kids to be Chia Pets and it's unrealistic. For one thing, I make mistakes in front of them. Half the time it's intentional, the other half, I really just made a mistake. I'm comfortable with that and I show them it's not a big deal. I'm human. I try to foster growth by praising mistakes. If a kid answers wrong, it's okay. It's awesome because it gives us an opportunity to think it through and talk about why you said what you said. Mistakes are stepping-stones. If none of us made mistakes, I wouldn't need to be an educator. There would be no need for schools. My classroom exists because we make mistakes.

Thinking: Strength and Conditioning

ow that a foundation for Knowing has been laid in Part I, we are ready to dive into Thinking. Meet Lucy Hale.

Hale has led a number of science-based cultural institutions across the state of Texas. She began her career as a live animal biologist at the Fort Worth Museum of Science and History before becoming the education manager at the Dallas Zoo and then the director of School Programs at Perot Museum of Nature and Science. In these capacities, Hale has developed a crucial appreciation for employees who can differentiate between Knowledge and Understanding, which you will remember as the first two levels of Bloom's Taxonomy.

According to Hale, "knowledgeable" zoo and museum employees should be capable of rapidly retrieving information while working with live animals. But, the best employees can also

Small Teaching K–8

apply their "understanding" in practical situations to ensure the well-being of the animals as well as one another. In other words, you can learn everything there is to know about a mountain lion from a book, but understanding how to feed a mountain lion its dinner is a whole other ball game.

"There's an academic side to zookeeping," Hale explained. "Most people have degrees in biology, zoology, or animal science. They've learned the natural history of the animal they are working with. They know about its behaviors in the wild, what it eats, grooming routines, mating rituals, and so on. The animal, however, has not done the reading."

Hale will never forget one of her very first jobs, caring for alligators that had been confiscated as illegal pets. "It is commonly known that alligators can't jump on land," she said. "And so, whenever we received a new alligator, we would place it on the dry floor to be measured safely, until, one day—it jumped," she said.

One of her colleagues turned to the other biologists in disbelief and declared, "But, alligators can't jump."

Hale's boss rolled his eyes. "Well, this alligator obviously didn't study from the same textbook you did," he said. "Shame on you for not properly restraining the animal the whole time." The experience stuck with her.

"Saying an animal can only jump so high is like saying a human can only run so fast," Hale told me. "Your calculations might be true until you meet Sha'Carri Richardson or Usain Bolt, and then you'll have to readjust your expectations."

Part I of *Small Teaching K–8* is devoted to convincing you that time spent acquiring basic knowledge is worthwhile. The internet can provide students with vast quantities of information, but it cannot build a complex network of knowledge inside their brains. (At least, not yet.) Having a knowledge network is pivotal. The network provides the foundation for higher orders of thinking. The first three chapters of the book therefore focus on helping

74

students adopt effective routines and strategies to gain a strong foundation for knowledge.

The next step is teaching students to apply their knowledge far and wide through a range of cognitive activities. The following chapters provide a set of small teaching tools for strengthening classroom or virtual learning experiences and deepening under-standing to help students become mindful practitioners of their own thinking skills. As was the case with Hale's jumping alligator, there are bound to be surprises. Bring them on. The more students can practice taking risks with your coaching and guidance, the easier it will be for them to activate their knowledge and apply it to the real world on their own.

Chapter 5

Synthesizing

In order to strengthen and condition students' minds, we must help them recognize relationships and connections. Seeing potential connections between two concepts comes naturally to a group of people I call "the synthesizers." The synthesizers I know have no trouble looking at two seemingly unrelated things and recognizing the value they have to one another. You probably have a synthesizer or two in your class right now. They are not necessarily the highest achievers, but they are likely the best networkers. They bring out the value in others and elevate learning for everyone. With the right strategies and a fair amount of practice, anyone can learn to be a synthesizer.

When I was first introduced to the unbelievably talented public art consultant, Che Anderson, I was surprised to learn that he was not, nor has he ever been, an artist. Anderson is a key organizer of multiple arts festivals, including the POW! WOW! International Mural Festivals, The Governors Ball Music Festival, and the BLKOUT Walls Festival. In addition, he has led collaborative initiatives with a long list of brands such as Nike, Puma, Sprite, and Samsung. Anderson's value hinges on recognizing talent, building relationships, and connecting compatible creatives with one another. He is a legend of the public art world, but it is rare he ever wields a can of paint.

I have never met anyone better at forging relationships with creatives than Anderson. I've heard many of the biggest street artists in the world sing his praises. As a volunteer at a POW! WOW! Festival in 2019, I found myself 30 feet up on a lift, priming a brick wall with Mississippi muralist Michael "Birdcap" Roy. "He might not be an artist, but he lives in our world," Roy (2019) told me of Anderson. "He has the respect of this community because we know we couldn't do what we love if we didn't have organizers like Che to take care of everything else."

Anderson is no stranger to municipal permits, social media engagement, volunteer coordination, and general hobnobbing. He makes sure artists like Birdcap can just show up and paint. Moreover, Anderson has established a complex network of knowledge about what it takes to plan and execute a festival. When he meets a new artist, scouts a new city, or courts a new sponsor—he simply slots the fresh information into place. Anderson is a professional synthesizer.

Malcolm Gladwell has another word for synthesizers; he calls them connectors. In his debut book *The Tipping Point*, Gladwell compares connectors to a computer network. Connectors feel comfortable making introductions among people from different social, economic, cultural, and professional circles. They see intersections as opportunities and thread ideas, concepts, and individuals together that might never otherwise cross.

Just as Che Anderson has never been a master painter, your students do not have to be mathematicians or Nobel Prize winners to establish a vast network of organized connections. Explicitly teaching students to determine main ideas, create concept maps, and fill in a framework will make them better synthesizers both in and outside of your class. Synthesis also lends itself to peer learning opportunities. Together, your students will build rich and productive networks of knowledge to take on the real world.

WHAT'S THE THEORY?

Allow me to oversimplify a complex subject here, if only for a few sentences, as we pause to appreciate what a tremendous privilege it is to change children's brains. There are two ways in which people learn. We can form new neuronal networks in our brains or modify the existing ones. Biologist James Zull estimates the brain has 100 million neurons, all of which "make friends easily" (2002, p. 96). Each new sensation, action, and thought produces a fresh connection in your neuronal network. The more you repeat that experience, the more defined the pathway becomes. A piece of knowledge that you reflect on and apply over various contexts will form connections to many neuronal networks in your brain. Maybe a song or a funny YouTube video reminds you of the information just learned, and bingo—you are connecting and synthesizing the two exposures to the information and creating a pathway. Each new use of that information adds another layer of the relationship until you achieve understanding.

Most synthesizers possess a strong working memory. In Chapter 1, I mentioned that a mature working memory, no matter how strong, can generally hold four new pieces of information at once. The difference between individuals with strong working memories and weak working memories is that a strong working memory can hold four robust pieces of information surrounded by a lot of context. That context is derived from prior knowledge held in the learner's long-term memory. A weak working memory has a much more difficult time establishing context and therefore struggles to move information from the working memory to the long-term memory.

In the book *Uncommon Sense Teaching: Practical Insights in Brain Science to Help Students Learn*, authors Barbara Oakley, Beth Rogowsky, and Terry Sejnowski describe the working memory as a four-armed octopus (2021). The octopus, more accurately a quadropus, can juggle four balls at once. If the octopus gets distracted, or tries to juggle too many balls at once, balls will fall to the ground—escaping the working memory. Retrieval practice makes the octopus a more skillful juggler. Once the information is well practiced and secured in the long-term memory, the octopus can begin juggling bigger and heavier balls of information. Oakley, Rogowsky, and Sejnowski remind us that the long-term memory has a vast capacity. "People's real problem with memory isn't how much they can store," they contend. "It's getting the information into or out of memory" (2021). They liken our brains to a music streaming service with millions upon millions of songs—our long-term memories help us locate the songs we are looking for by forming and organizing connections. The easier it becomes to retrieve the information we are looking for, the more connections we are able to make.

How People Learn, a 2000 publication of the National Research Council, compares the modification of neuronal networks to an artist chiseling a sculpture. "The nervous system sets up a large number of connections; experience then plays on this network, selecting the appropriate connections and removing the inappropriate ones." As you increase the number of relevant connections and help students synthesize information by identifying relationships, the sculpture becomes clearer. It is possible for existing networks to cause misinterpretations, but small teaching will help you to chisel away poor connections and replace them with rich new networks for learning.

In education, our goal is to help students build rich and overlapping frameworks of knowledge in each of the content areas. An ability to synthesize multiple frameworks allows students to connect and organize information for efficiency and application. As teachers, we help them learn to make connections for themselves. Experts make more connections than novices, so our job is to help facilitate deep synthesis of information across many contexts. Unfortunately, we cannot fire the synapses in our students' brains for them. They have to synthesize the information on their own in a way that makes sense to them.

According to *How Learning Works: 7 Research-Based Principles for Smart Teaching*, the difference between experts and novices often hinges on "the number or density of connections among the concepts, facts, and skills they know" (Ambrose, Bridges, DiPietro, Lovett, and Norman, 2010, p. 49). A novice's web of understanding contains holes that inevitably impact comprehension. On the contrary, an expert is capable of weaving new information into a fibrous canvas of connections, which then become more stable and more easily activated in multiple contexts. The more an expert can tie newly acquired facts to previous knowledge, the easier it becomes to apply their knowledge in fresh ways.

That said, please never make the assumption that your students lack all prior knowledge of something you are attempting to teach them. Intelligence is malleable. Trust that as soon as you introduce a new concept, their brains will begin searching for connections in an attempt to synthesize whatever they already know with whatever you are telling them. Similar to prediction, activating prior knowledge will give you a better idea of misconceptions and realistic entry points for the children sitting in front of you.

IN SHORT

- The more an experience is repeated, the more defined it will become in your long-term memory.
- Every time you use a piece of information in a new way, you are creating a new point of connection in your long-term memory.
- The working memory can hold up to four new pieces of information at one time. As they are transferred to the long-term memory, the working memory becomes capable of holding bigger and more robust chunks of new information.

- The long-term memory is vast; space is not an issue. The real challenge is organizing enormous amounts of information to make it easily accessible on demand.
- Possessing prior content knowledge will help a learner to master a new skill more easily, even if it is a content-neutral skill.
- Experts have a dense network of connections in their long-term memories while novices have holes in their network that need to be filled in.
- As soon as a new piece of information is introduced, the brain begins searching for relevant connections in the long-term memory.

MODELS

In Massachusetts, where I teach, the state test began requiring students to write their open response essays based on two sources rather than one in 2015. Pretty soon, everyone became obsessed with the term *synthesis*. It was no longer enough to provide text evidence from multiple readings; students needed to establish a relationship between the readings if they wanted to earn top marks.

I recently had a conversation with the English Department Head in my building, Kerry Trotto, to ask her how she handled the shift with her students. She told me her lifeline had been a text called *Notice & Note: Strategies for Close Reading* by Kylene Beers and Robert E. Probst (2012). "At the time, our entire teaching faculty completed a book study focused on the 'Notice and Note' signposts in order to create common reading strategies used throughout the building rather than just in English classes," Trotto (2021) recalled. "This book study allowed teachers to use the same bank of reading strategies and common language in classes so that students could practice the strategies with a variety of texts throughout all content areas."

In addition, Trotto expressed gratitude for professional development on the Self-Regulated Strategy Development (SRSD) writing program. "In the same manner as the reading strategies and terms, another set of common language and strategies was created for all teachers to use with their students for writing tasks," she said. "The addition of the SRSD strategies was helpful for teaching students to synthesize two texts by following the routines of the program." Students became accustomed to engaging in "self-talk," a process we explored at length in Chapter 2. They also practiced pulling apart writing prompts strategically to figure out what the question required them to do. "Students were taught how to write a HOT introduction paragraph that included a hook, overview, and thesis," shared Trotto. "Emphasis was put on writing a strong thesis statement that we referred to as the 'heart of the essay'." With the use of common reading and writing strategies across all classes, she found the shift toward synthesizing two texts took place for most students with relative ease.

Synthesis comes naturally to some students, but I find that many of my high achievers have the most difficult time making the adjustment. It turns out, being able to recall every state capital off the top of your head does not equate to crafting an in-depth analysis of a state capital's assets based on multiple primary sources. You get the idea. Memorization only takes you so far.

Synthesis should be happening in your classroom year-round. The five models included here will help students build connections and recognize relationships from the first day of school through their final report cards.

Synthesis Sentence Starters

In the Beers and Probst text recommended by my colleague Kerry Trotto, the authors recommend instituting "generalizable language" or "signposts" that can be repeated frequently and applied to many, if not all, texts (2012, p. 85). The standardized sign-posts include:

- *Contrast and Contradictions:* When a character acts in an unexpected way, pause and ask yourself, "Why would the character act this way?" Start your answer with, "As I think about this question, I wonder if it might be . . ."
- *Aha Moment:* When a character realizes something, ask yourself, "How might this change things?" Start your answer with, "Now that this character realizes this, I think that . . ."
- *Tough Questions:* When a character asks himself or a friend a difficult question, you get a glimpse of what is bothering him the most. Stop and ask yourself, "What does this question make me wonder about?" Start your answer with, "These questions he was asking himself make me think that . . ."
- *Words of the Wiser:* When an older or more experienced character shares advice, ask yourself, "What's the life lesson and how might it affect the character?" Start your answer with, "The important lesson offered here is that . . ."
- *Again and Again:* When you see repetition, something is important. You have to ask yourself, "Why does this keep happening again and again?" Start your answer with, "Here I see . . ."
- *Memory Moment:* The memory of the past can be used to explain the present moment. Stop and ask yourself, "Why might the memory be important? Start your answer with, "The memory seems important because . . ."

It is important to use consistent language in order to provide students with a common context through which to view connections. By hanging anchor charts around your classroom, learning becomes more visible. Anchor charts are large print, student-generated reference posters that are easy to point to as a scaffold throughout the year. By asking students to create the charts themselves, they begin to feel a sense of ownership over the material as well as their physical learning space.

Aside from the *Notice & Note* signposts detailed earlier, the anchor chart I rely on most heavily is a list of synthesis sentence starters designed to help students craft their open responses. Given that synthesis does not come naturally to the vast majority of learners, I like to give students a jump start by encouraging them to use sentence starters such as:

According to both . . .

At first, I thought . . . but now I think . . . because . . .

This makes me think of . . .

I know synthesis is taking place when students are able to take two or more concepts or sources and articulate a meaningful connection. When this language becomes ingrained in the majority of my students' responses, I can replace the synthesis anchor chart with something new. The students who are still struggling with synthesis receive their own copy of the sentence starters to tape inside their desk or on the back of their digital device.

Another great strategy for synthesis is the summary frame: "Somebody, wanted, but, so, then" (Beers, 2003). For example, to summarize *Harry Potter and the Sorcerer's Stone* by J. K. Rowling, I would write, "Voldemort wanted the Sorcerer's Stone, but Harry was determined to protect it, so he snuck to the forbidden third-floor corridor, then he outsmarted his mortal enemy." Different students are sure to come up with unique configurations.

Once students have mastered summarizing a single reading, you can ask them to use the "somebody, wanted, but, so, then" frame for two readings. For example, to synthesize *Harry Potter and the Sorcerer's Stone* with *The Lightning Thief* by Rick Riordan, I could write: "Both heroes wanted to avenge their parents, but they needed to find a powerful tool, so they teamed up with friends and then returned victorious." Here, the framing device is the same, but students are asked to consider two sources rather than one, thereby identifying significant connections and relationships in both texts.

The more an experience is repeated, the more defined it becomes in the long-term memory. Therefore, instituting generalizable language with which students can consistently approach reading makes it easier for them to form important connections. Posting sentence starters and sentence frames throughout your classroom is the easiest way to reinforce the practice of synthesis.

Knowledge Dumps

The first "photo dump" I saw on Instagram came from Ariana Grande in December 2020. Grande announced her wedding engagement with a mirror selfie, some blurry outtakes of her fiancé on a hardwood floor, and a picture of a diamond ring perched on her tattooed finger. The *New York Times*'s Styles Desk followed soon after with a "close reading" of the engagement that proclaimed, "In 2020, a year so hellish that the old rules of Instagram could no longer apply, a new format surged in popularity: the photo dump. . . . It's how Ariana Grande announced her engagement and also how most internet-savvy celebrities have been posting for months now" (2020). Photo dumps flew in the face of highly curated Instagram feeds—a standard practice of the "before times." Quarantine led to carousels of varied and mundane pandemic shots as we baked our sourdough loaves and learned to tie-dye at home.

Photo dumps feel more intimate and revealing than the staged posts of our pre-pandemic lives because they provide a random collection of images, not a curated one. As a result, it's up to the viewer to synthesize the images on their own. Everyone who views the same photo dump can draw their own conclusions, create their own unique interpretation, and generate their own synthesis.

Knowledge dumps do the same, asking students to share everything they know (or think they know) about a topic before you teach them. Prior knowledge can then be reinforced, and misconceptions can be squashed.

Like the carousel feature on Instagram that allows users to post 10 photos for their followers to swipe through, I conduct carousels in my classroom. I post six pieces of chart paper throughout the room with broad guiding questions and distribute students among them. They begin by scrawling their answers on the chart paper in front of them and every couple of minutes, they rotate to the next piece of chart paper. Eventually, they circulate all the way around the room. Some teachers call this activity "chalk talk" and conduct the brain dump silently on the board, though I haven't seen an actual blackboard with chalk in over a decade. Once you process the knowledge your students dumped, you can allow the information you've collected to inform future instructional approaches.

Brain dumps can be used to teach everything from multiplication and division to good citizenship. I have found a lot of success with The KIDS (Kids Involved Doing Service Learning) Consortium activity for building an effective citizen. On the first day of class, students are split into groups and given silhouettes of various parts of a human body, including the head, hands, heart, and feet. The group members work together to populate each body part with a brain dump depicting the behaviors of an effective citizen. On the head, they might write, "Think before you speak" or "Do your research." In the hands they might write, "Extends a helping hand" or "Hard working." In the heart might write "Courageous" or "Proud." And so on.

I can detect a lot from the effective citizen brain dump, including who my concrete and abstract learners are. Do they understand idioms? Can they assign symbolism? Have they received prior character education? By asking what they already know, I am able to tailor the course to my students' collective and individual needs. Likewise, students do their own valuable synthesis work of drawing conclusions and creating unique interpretations.

Finding the Main Idea

I lived in more than a dozen homes before graduating high school. Silver linings are few and far between when it comes to housing insecurity, but I did become a very good packer. I learned that if you put a book, a toothbrush, and a spatula in a box and label it "stuff," you're going to have a hell of a time unpacking. It's much easier to fill a well-labeled box for each room with similar items. This strategy, based on Keys to Literacy, is how I teach students to find the main idea.

I start with literal examples. "If I packed a blender, silverware, and a coffee mug in a box, what would I label it?" I ask them. Most kids catch on right away: "Kitchen!" Next, I move to more abstract examples. "If I put a slice of pizza, a pine tree, and the Eiffel Tower in a box, what would I label it?" It usually takes them longer to arrive at something suitable like "triangles." Finally, I give them a label of my choosing and ask what they would put in the box. If I say, "Landforms," they might respond with, "hills, volcanoes, and peninsulas."

Practice Packing Boxes:

Label each box below by identifying the main ideas and details.

Blender	Eiffel Tower
Silverware	Slice of Pizza
Coffee Mug	Pine Tree
Label:	**Label:**
1.	1.
2.	2.
3.	3.
Label: Living Room	**Label:**

Main Idea	Details
	1.
	2.
	3.
	1.
	2.
	3.
	1.
	2.
	3.
	1.
	2.
	3.
	1.
	2.
	3.
	1.
	2.
	3.

I rarely provide students with a completed copy of my notes or presentations. Once they get the hang of labeling main ideas, I begin providing them with a skeleton of my notes riddled with strategic blanks. The notes are split into two columns: main ideas and details, establishing a hierarchy of key concepts. This strategy helps them fill in the blanks in their neural networks and build accurate connections.

Similar to the knowledge dump technique, finding relationships among details to establish the main idea is a simple path to synthesis. As novice learners, I recognize they would likely struggle to organize their own notes into main ideas and details. By providing a structure for meaningful note-taking, I can gradually release the responsibility until students are able to identify most main ideas and details on their own.

Concept Maps

At the end of a lesson or unit, I like to ask students to design a concept map. Google's free Jamboard platform is a great digital tool for concept mapping, but paper and pencil will work just fine. Concept maps look the way they sound, a visual web of main ideas and key details with connecting lines to represent relationships.

Concept maps are graphic representations, usually organized in a hierarchy, introducing the most general ideas at the top with increasingly specific details or concepts as one move's down the page. The map denotes relationships between various ideas, details, and concepts. Researchers Joseph D. Novak and Alberto J. Cañas praise the practice of concept mapping, noting, "There is still relatively little known about memory processes and how knowledge finally gets incorporated into our brain, but it seems evident from diverse sources of research that our brain works to organize knowledge in hierarchical frameworks and that learning approaches that facilitate this process significantly enhance the learning capability of all learners" (2008). Concept maps provide the brain with a template to begin moving new information from the working memory to the long-term memory. Remember, the long-term memory is vast; space is not an issue. The real challenge is organizing enormous amounts of information to make it easily accessible on demand.

Interviewed for Jennifer Gonzalez's popular *Cult of Pedagogy* podcast, Amanda Cardenas recommends thinking of your concept map as a vision board. Cardenas is an English teacher and independent consultant based out of Chicago. "A unit vision board is a lesson planning tool that allows teachers to imagine their units as an experience and think through what it would *feel like* to be part of that experience," explains Cardenas (2021). Cardenas provides an example in which she places the essential question in the center of a Google Slide, accompanied by a corresponding YouTube video, images, a color scheme appropriate to the tone of the unit, major themes, and the most significant anchor quotes from assigned reading. "Could I have accomplished this on our department issued spreadsheet?" she asks. "Sure. But a spreadsheet with bullets and columns is a little less . . . alive" (2021). I recommend creating your own concept map prior to asking your students to do the same.

Concept maps make great collaborative activities. I often ask students to choose among four roles in their groups: Main Ideator, Dr. Detail, Connector, and Discussion Leader. The Main Ideator generates a list of main ideas from the unit. Then, Dr. Detail records at least three details for each of the main ideas. The Connector draws lines to show the relationships between main ideas and details. The Discussion Leader keeps time and tracks the participation of all group members. In the end, we take a gallery walk to see what everyone else comes up with. Students post their maps throughout the room and take time to circulate, leaving comments on sticky notes for the other groups.

Asking a focused question to guide the concept map is an excellent way to get started. A social studies teacher might ask, "What were the positive and negative consequences of the American Revolution?" While, a science teacher might ask, "What's the difference between three types of matter?" Sorting main ideas and details on a concept map will build a denser network of connections and strengthen the synthesis of multiple topics or themes. By the end of the year, students should be able to turn your course syllabus into a concept map of its own.

The Minute Thesis

Jim Lang's approach to synthesis in his college literature courses benefits from an original strategy he calls, "The Minute Thesis." At the end of each semester, Lang writes every title from his syllabus in one column on the board and a list of themes in a second column. Next, he asks a student to circle a single theme and draw connecting lines to at least two of the novels. Students have one minute to develop a thesis statement connecting the two novels to the theme. Fascinating new connections and relationships emerge in a class discussion for 5–10 minutes before he begins the process again with new selections.

Lang has implemented this activity in anywhere from 10-minute chunks to an entire class period. Like many of the teaching strategies he champions, The Minute Thesis is free, easy, and appropriate for any class size. He recalls the first time he tried The Minute Thesis in the original edition of *Small Teaching*:

> I wrote the name of the seven novels we had read on the board in a single column; in a second column, I wrote a list of themes that we had seen in various novels throughout the semester. I handed a marker to a student in the front row, asked her to walk up to the board and circle a single

theme, and then asked her to draw lines connecting that theme to two different novels. Then I asked the students to spend 1 minute thinking about a thesis for an argument that would explain how those two novels connected to that theme. (2016)

Lang was impressed by the sophisticated thesis statements that emerged from his students. He hadn't previously thought to tackle the "mysterious process of coming up with new or original ideas" head on. The Minute Thesis helped Lang target a skill he had asked his students to apply constantly by writing papers, delivering presentations, and completing research projects. New and original ideas are most often just creative connections. "Playing the minute thesis demystifies the process of coming up with new connections," Lang points out, "and gives the students a tool they can use in all of their classes when they are trying to brainstorm ideas for their assignments" (2016). After all, every time you use a piece of information in a new way, you are creating a new point of connection in your long-term memory.

PRINCIPLES

Exercises in synthesis require you to throw your expert rope to novice students in order to help them identify relationships among multiple concepts. The easier it becomes for them to determine main ideas and compose summary statements, the simpler it will be for them to create their own connections to content. In like manner, the more prior content knowledge students possess in their long-term memories, the easier it will be for them to apply new skills such as determining main ideas and composing summaries.

Provide the Framework

As a content expert, you are able to organize new information with ease. You can connect concepts and detect meaningful relationships within the complex neuronal network of your long-term memory. New learners need a lot of help with organization. A strong and visible framework should clearly state goals, concepts, and materials for your unit. Refer to the framework frequently so students can begin to build networks of their own. The more familiar students are with your unit plan or syllabus, the easier it will become for them to fit new information into the frame.

Facilitate Synthesis

Even if students someday rise to your level of content expertise, their networks will look different than yours. The frame you have provided them with is filled with empty space for a reason. As they build their own connections and relationships, their learning grows deeper. Provide ample opportunity for students to establish surprising juxtapositions and explore new pathways between concepts.

Leverage Peer Learning

Synthesis is a natural outlet for collaborative group work because it requires relationship building. All of your students are novice learners, but together, they can forge new pathways by helping each other. Group work can be productive and energizing for students in addition to encouraging natural curiosity to flourish.

SMALL TEACHING QUICK TIPS: SYNTHESIS

Synthesizing two concepts is much more difficult than retrieving or memorizing a single piece of information. Devoting precious time to skills such as finding the main idea and summarizing may require an investment on your part, but students will reap the benefits in the long term. Learning to examine the relationship between multiple pieces of information contributes to deeper and longer-lasting learning.

- Provide students with sentence starters and sentence frames to familiarize them with the language of synthesis. Post anchor charts throughout your classroom to make learning visible. Start with: "At first, I thought . . . but now I think . . . because . . ." Next, encourage students to write succinct summaries using a sentence frame such as "somebody, wanted, but, so then."
- Pry for prior knowledge with a brain dump activity at the start of the unit to establish an entry-point for students to begin synthesizing multiple concepts or sources.
- Ask students to answer a guiding question by creating a concept map made up of main ideas and details that connect to one another.
- Use a packing box to illustrate the process of finding the main idea. Students should learn to label a box filled with silverware, a blender, and plates: "kitchen." Next, fill the box with details from a unit of study and see if they can determine how to label it.
- Use The Minute Thesis activity to help students recognize and create new connections prior to major assignments or exams.

CONCLUSION

As a master of synthesis, public art consultant Che Anderson has grown accustomed to asking the question, "Can it translate?" When making connections to grow his network, he has to gauge compatibility. What will happen when two artists, concepts, or resources collide? Will they enhance one another? I imagine

Anderson like a telephone switchboard operator from the 1940s, toggling between wires to bring the right people together. "Someone might have gone to a great art school," he told me, "But, that doesn't mean they will be able to translate their work into a mural" (Anderson, 2021).

You have probably experienced a diligent student like this in your classroom who has done the homework, but flounders when asked to connect it to something you taught earlier in the year. It is easy to look at the individual plots outlined by Author A, Author B, and Author C. It becomes much harder to establish a common theme among them. Novice learners rarely engage in synthesis without prompting the way you, as a content expert, likely do. The more information they move into their long-term memories, the easier it becomes to make connections and synthesize new material.

Provide students with a concrete framework for learning and they will eventually begin to make connections among ideas, concepts, and texts. Encourage them to examine main ideas independently before trying to establish how two things are related. Sometimes allowing novice students to work in a group can illuminate connections even you, as the expert, could not see before.

Chapter 6

Practicing

S ometimes I still forget I am not the main character in my own classroom. The more time I spend talking, the less effective my lessons often become. Application and practice are pivotal elements of learning, and I can do neither of them for my students. They have to put in the effort themselves. That said, observing their practice helps to guide my teaching and helps me make effective adjustments to practice. The more frequently I facilitate short practice sessions, the better students perform on my assessments.

It's easy to feel guilty when you allow students to do all the talking. Whenever my administrators walk into the room and students are actively engaged with one another, I have to remind myself not to interject for the sole purpose of demonstrating my own importance or value. Administrators want to see students reaching for the higher levels of Bloom's Taxonomy and to do that, they have to make a little noise. Practice sessions are not a time for teachers to be passive, the same way your classroom is not a place for your students to passively absorb information from you. Learn to give meaningful feedback that requires students to take action and model that skill for your students on a regular basis.

Placing your students in a variety of new contexts and environments, and then asking them to practice and apply the skills you've taught them is a pivotal part of transferring information from short-term memory to long-term memory. I found practice sessions particularly necessary with the digitization of standardized exams. When our state test went digital, I realized there were very basic skills I had taken for granted. One girl came to me in tears because she hadn't been able to scroll down during the test. Her academic skills were phenomenal but her technology skills were limited. I began reserving the Chromebook cart regularly and digitized all of my assessments. Whatever skills I planned to assess for a grade, we practiced in class—even things as simple as navigating a scroll bar.

I sought out the Deputy Commissioner of the Massachusetts Department of Elementary and Secondary Education at the time, Jeff Wulfson, to ask about the decision to go digital. "This was a mega-project to totally redesign our tests to make sure they're fully aligned with and demonstrating deep understanding of the curriculum standards that we have updated over the last several years," Wulfson told me, adding, "Computer-based testing was just one facet of that. These are all new tests, new questions, new ways of assessing student performance" (2019).

Wulfson recalled an environment just a few years ago when computer labs with 20 workstations for periodic class visits were the norm across the state of Massachusetts. He viewed this practice as antiquated, replaced by an increased volume of one-to-one computing environments in which every student was issued a laptop or a tablet.

"We think that's a great development and an important one that computer-based testing was just the sort of little push that districts needed to get that done," Wulfson said (2021).

My opinion on dedicating time to test-taking skills is sometimes unpopular. I believe test-taking skills are life skills. Want to obtain a driver's license? You'll have to pass a test on a computer. Want to become an accountant? You'll have to pass a test on a computer. Want to work as an electrician? You'll have to pass a test on a computer. I admit there's more to it than just learning to drag and drop or sort through multiple choice questions. Still, learning to take tests is a surefire path to upward mobility. My students found digital test-taking to be radically different from taking a test with pencil and paper. Explicitly outlining those discrepancies for students, and practicing the motor and cognitive skills necessary to be successful made a huge difference.

"We don't want people to spend too much time on test prep; we don't think that's productive," Wulfson told me. "It's more important that they spend time studying the curriculum and learning the material, but there are some tools available to familiarize them with the computer-based testing platform" (2021). As Wulfson suggested, the practice tests provided by the state's Testing Resource Center proved a great place to familiarize students with tech-driven skills, prior to the summative exam. It quickly became apparent to me that students who could transfer test-taking skills to the screen were far more likely to succeed.

Digital testing isn't going anywhere; in fact, the ability to test on a screen is becoming a life skill. The College Board now offers a digital SAT. As it stands, most careers administer licensure exams digitally. In July 2019, the Law School Admission Test partnered with Microsoft to begin offering a digital LSAT. Whether you aim to become a lawyer, doctor, plumber, or bail bondsman, you've got to pass a computer-based test. Practice makes perfect.

WHAT'S THE THEORY?

Retrieving, introduced in Chapter 1, is also a form of practice. In this chapter, we discuss how practice strengthens higher level skills and allows for retrieval in brand-new environments. A distinct feature of this chapter, different from retrieval, is the art of delivering effective feedback to create more mindful practice for students applying familiar information in an unfamiliar context.

Harvard psychologist Ellen Langer is a huge proponent of mindful learning. Langer defines a mindful approach to teaching with three characteristics: "the continuous creation of new categories; openness to new information; and an implicit awareness of more than one perspective" (Langer, 1997, p. 4). A mindful learner does not depend on formulaic thinking. A mindful learner applies new information and seeks fresh angles and perspectives with which to approach already familiar information. Most importantly, a mindful learner accepts the possibility that new approaches and conclusions are imminent while maintaining an attitude of openness.

"It is virtually impossible to become proficient at a mental task," wrote cognitive psychologist Daniel Willingham, "without extended practice" (Willingham 2014, p. 107). Willingham further explains that the act of thinking requires students to combine information from their environments and their memories in new ways (p. 109). Willingham draws on the ability of math students who have memorized their multiplication tables. These students waste no energy or brainpower on calculating simple multiplication, thereby saving space in their working memories to tackle more complex problems. Willingham writes, "It is no wonder that students who have memorized facts do better in all sorts of math tasks than students whose knowledge of math tasks is absent or uncertain. And it's been shown that practicing math facts helps low-achieving students do better on more advanced mathematics" (2014, p. 114). This is because the potential to think is not unlimited; the working memory eventually reaches capacity. By practicing a cognitive skill, humans are able to achieve a state of automaticity, thereby saving space in their working memories for new information.

Football player Dexter McCluster offers an excellent example of physical automaticity. By McCluster's senior year at Ole Miss, he had earned a reputation as the only player in SEC history to rush for over 1,000 yards and receive for 500 yards in a single season. In 2010, he was drafted by the Kansas City Chiefs in the second round and went on to play in the 2013 Pro Bowl. I asked McCluster about his career highlight and without skipping a beat he answered:

> My punt return against the New York Giants. It was kind of surreal. I was on the field making the moves, but I don't know how my body was doing it, you know? I was back deep. I made the spin. Made one guy miss. Made a couple more guys miss. Then, I took it to the house. That was a pivotal moment in the game. And it was just one of those highlights where when I watched the replay I said, 'How do I do that?' My body just took over (2019).

McCluster put in countless hours of practice to arrive at that moment. He wasted no energy because his body knew what it had to do. He had achieved automaticity.

Like the football player who commits to an arduous practice regimen leading up to game day, our students require regular practice sessions prior to summative assessments. Even so, there is a risk of overlearning. If the football player becomes so accustomed to a practice regimen that he begins to mindlessly go through the motions, the benefits will be few and far between. Similarly, a student drilled to the point of autopilot will prevent them from refining and further developing their skills.

How can learners benefit from automaticity without overlearning? Practice and feedback. There's a reason football players practice under the guidance of a coach and teammates. Similarly, students should not be left to their own devices to practice. Peer and teacher feedback is the key to mindful learning.

Bowman Dickson and Andy Housiaux outline four "big ideas" for effective feedback in a 2021 report for Tang Institute. Their findings intend to support teachers distressed by the feeling that students are not taking the time to even read the feedback they take hours to provide. Unfortunately, a teacher's level of effort does not directly translate to a student's meaningful takeaways.

The first idea championed by Dickson and Housiaux proclaims, "Students must engage with feedback in order to learn from it" (2021). They believe it is well worth the sacrifice to dedicate class time for students to process and respond to teacher comments. It's also important to remember that feedback will be received differently by different students. Interacting with feedback might mean students annotate your comments with a plus and delta system to indicate positives (plus) and areas for improvement (delta). Older students might be asked to respond to each piece of teacher feedback in writing before making edits to their own work.

Dickson and Housiaux's second idea states, "Feedback depends on a student's identity and their relationship to their teacher" (2021). They urge teachers to consider their own power positions such as gender and race, which could be triggering for students. In classroom cultures where mistakes are valued as part of learning, teachers were more effective in the role of *warm demander*, a term coined by Zaretta Hammond. Dickson and Housiaux clarify, "A warm demander doesn't overpraise mediocre work, but holds high standards for all students and supports them while they progress toward them" (2021).

The third big idea from Dickson and Housiaux states, "Quality feedback focuses on specific instructional goals" (2021). Keep your comments pointed and narrow to the task. If you taught a lesson on apostrophes this week, don't bother marking up a student's paper with a million spelling corrections. Only give feedback on their apostrophe use. Comments should be targeted; you don't have to write a novel. Your feedback is not meant to turn back time and correct every error made during a student's first attempt at a new skill. Feedback is meant to meaningfully shape future approaches. Take it one step at a time.

Finally, Dickson and Housiaux's fourth big idea reminds teachers, "Feedback and grading are different" (2021). The grade you give is not an effective form of feedback. Students should be asked to grapple with your feedback before you determine their final grades. In an ideal world, students become more invested in your feedback than their final grade.

Using precious class time for "practice" can sometimes feel wasteful. As teachers, we are in constant conversation with ourselves, asking: "Is this the best use of my educational expertise?" When it comes to guided practice, the answer is yes. This is not a self-directed activity or an opportunity for teachers to catch up on emails. Practice sessions rely on a teacher to provide feedback and play the role of coach.

In the models that follow, we explore simple ways to strengthen and condition the mind to maximize learning outcomes for students who practice.

IN SHORT

- Mastering a mental task requires practice in a variety of contexts. Practice retrieving and categorizing information in a variety of environments (digital and analog) and from multiple viewpoints.
- Memorizing a piece of information by practicing it over and over in the same way does not guarantee you will be able to recall it in a brand-new context.
- Recognize formulaic thinking and the sensation of "going through the motions." Should this occur, seek out a fresh angle with which you approach already familiar information.
- Peer and teacher feedback makes practice more meaningful and beneficial to the learner, particularly when students are asked to engage or interact with the feedback in some way.

- Consider your relationship with a student to determine the tone with which you deliver feedback as they practice a new skill. Remember, a grade is not the same thing as feedback.

MODELS

We have all met the brilliant kid who can write Shakespearean-level prose, but when asked to deliver an oral presentation, she crumbles under the pressure. Just because a student is gifted in one domain does not mean she will be capable of mastering any cognitive challenge thrown at her. It takes practice.

Practice is pretty straightforward. Do something over and over, making small adjustments along the way, until your body and mind can complete the task automatically and efficiently. Physical skills certainly benefit from practice, but so do cognitive skills. Make time for brief and regular opportunities to practice the cognitive skills that will help students perform successfully on assessments. Figure out students' intrinsic motivations and determine how they connect to the new skills you are asking them to practice. Allow for feedback from you or from peers before you assign a formal grade of any kind. The following three models intend to create ideal conditions for effective practice sessions.

Unpack Your Assessments

I always try to plan my lessons and units backward, prioritizing learning goals over activities. I plan assessments backward as well. I am constantly reminding myself that the priorities on my assessments should be the same priorities as the ones emphasized in my day-to-day instruction. By unpacking the assessments I administer to my students, I am able to determine what will be the most beneficial skills to practice during class time. It is often surprising how many things we expect to come naturally to our students that we never bother to teach.

For example, I once worked for a principal who insisted that every teacher conduct a lesson about how to walk down the hall during the first week of school. "How can we hold them accountable in the halls if we don't explicitly teach them our expectations?" he would say. My colleagues griped over the lost time-on-learning while we modeled "staying to the right" for our students, but I noticed an immediate uptick in positive hallway behaviors. I learned to never make assumptions, especially when it comes to what kids already know.

Take, for example, the beast of any middle school classroom— the five-paragraph essay. Students are expected to analyze a question, develop an outline, cite evidence, and write with style—usually in less than an hour's time. Zoom in closer and you'll find a barrage of difficult skills are required to successfully complete the assignment:

· Composing an introductory paragraph
· Crafting a thesis or claim
· Integrating relevant quotations
· Transitioning between body paragraphs
· Delivering a conclusion

I'm sure I could come up with a dozen more skills that a complex five-paragraph essay calls for, but you get the idea. Depending on the objective, you might value one of these skills far above the rest. That is the skill you should be practicing during class on a regular basis.

Students deserve an opportunity to practice before any high stakes assessments. One of my colleagues, Tracy Pobieglo, has gotten in the habit of providing her students with "choice" practice assessments in her middle school math classroom. Students can select the problems to complete from a bank and each is given a point value by complexity. The objective is to score the highest grade possible.

"Additionally, I have been using a strategy called 'Paper Talk,'" explained Pobieglo (2021). "Students work in a group, are given a problem, and then follow a set protocol for solving." Her protocol consists of two minutes for quiet thinking time to write on one side of a large piece of chart paper. Next, students have three minutes to share their thoughts followed by two minutes to finalize the group's answer in the middle of the large poster board.

"Last week, to assess how students were doing with comparing linear functions, I had them complete four practice stations worth of work as a group, and then at the end, they spent time individually practicing an analysis activity." All of Pobieglo's assessments mirror the types of problems completed in class, as well as the released state test questions. "I try to allow for some choice and I stagger the questions, gradually deepening in complexity as students move to the end of the assessment," she said (2021). Pobieglo always gives credit for showing work, even if the resulting solution is not accurate.

High school teachers will complain that students should have learned a particular skill in their middle school classes. Middle school teachers will complain they should have taught it in the intermediate grades. Intermediate teachers will say the primary teachers dropped the ball. The truth is, tackling a complex assessment takes a lifetime of practice. Break down your assessments into the smallest pieces you can, and identify the cognitive skills you intend to prioritize the highest. Those are the ones that merit practice time.

Parcel Them Out and Practice Them

Dedicating precious minutes to allow for regular practice sessions is absolutely an appropriate use of class time. In her mathematics classroom, Pobieglo uses an "I do, we do, you do" approach to practicing, ending classes with opportunities for independent application. "I use a lot of thinking aloud and point out to students that what I am saying aloud should be similar to the conversation they have with themselves when solving problems independently during practice time at the end of class" (2021). In addition, she posts an assignment every Monday that is due on the Friday of that week. "The homework is always based on a topic we have already done and serves as a spiraling review requiring them to practice old skills," she explained. By placing a high value on deliberate practice during class, Pobieglo's students can begin to see the value in practicing at home.

Practice sessions often come in the latter half of my own class because I find it to be the best opportunity for application and reinforcement. Following an in-class debate, for example, I would use the last 10 minutes of class to ask students to formulate a claim or thesis based on the lively arguments they have just presented for their peers. Even better, I could reserve 15 minutes at the end of class and spend 5 of those minutes reviewing the equation for a great thesis before asking students to compose their own thesis statements:

Author & Title + Firm Opinion + Most Compelling Evidence = Thesis

In Frank Stockton's short story "The Lady, or the Tiger?" the tiger emerges from the door because the princess is too jealous to see him love another.

At the start of the next class, I might begin by requiring students to locate a strong piece of text evidence to support their thesis:

How her soul had burned in agony when she had seen him rush to meet that woman, with her flushing cheek and sparkling eye of triumph; when she had seen him lead her forth, his whole frame kindled with the joy of recovered life . . . and when she had seen them walk away together upon their path of flowers, followed by the tremendous shouts of the hilarious multitude, in which her one despairing shriek was lost and drowned! (Stockton, 1882).

Next, I would ask students to pen a single body paragraph. As with the thesis, it might be worth reviewing the components of a strong body paragraph before we jump in:

· Topic Sentence
· Evidence
· Explanation
· Closing Sentence

The final product would look something like this:

In Frank Stockton's short story "The Lady, or the Tiger?" it is obvious the tiger emerges from the door because the princess is too jealous to see him love another. When the princess envisions her lover marrying someone else, Stockton writes, ". . . and when she had seen them walk away together upon their path of flowers, followed by the tremendous shouts of the hilarious multitude, in which her one despairing shriek was lost and drowned!" (1882). This reaction confirms that her semi-barbaric nature is too strong to allow the courtier to go on living if it means he will be with a fair maiden other than the princess. The princess' jealousy drives her decision to commit an unthinkable act, sentencing her lover to death.

Finally, I would ask students to label each part of their body paragraph to reinforce their recognition of each component.

Younger students might not be ready to practice an entire body paragraph, but they could certainly practice writing a topic sentence broken down into similar components.

Giving students weekly tasks like this to replicate a future assessment will help them build stamina and familiarity through practice before you administer a summative exam, essay, or project. In the case of an oral presentation, students might be asked to create a single "teaser" slide and a one-minute explanation to be used for practice in class, leading up to their final presentation. Practice "packing boxes." The main idea box from Chapter 5, is also an effective way for students to determine the main idea for each slide and develop a corresponding speaking point.

Encouraging your students to consider alternatives and backup plans is a surefire way to reinforce flexibility and creativity. Even if they feel confident about the status of their product, try to suggest redesigning the presentation for someone completely unfamiliar with your subject matter. Then, ask them what changed from their initial script. When kids tell me they are super confident and don't need to practice, I remind them that there is nothing worse than freezing up in front of an audience. I ask them to write out what they plan to say, just in case. More often than not, they thank me later.

Provide Feedback

Practice without feedback can be thankless, and lead to listless and boring repetition with very little benefit. The ideal practice-feedback loop happens in real-time. I often think of my favorite yoga teachers who gently correct my postures as I engage in my yoga practice. Over time, I am able to hold the postures on my own and recall their pointers from memory in order to tweak my body position based on their previous feedback.

Tutoring or extra help is a privilege enjoyed by many students, though they may not see it that way. Large class sizes prevent me from providing individualized feedback to every child every day. Alternatively, I rely on peer feedback as a means for enhancing practice sessions. While students work in pairs or groups to provide feedback, I circulate the room to address the needs of struggling students. During peer feedback, I like to provide "accountable talk" sentence starters to help students give one another feedback in a productive way.

Some basic sentence starters might include:

- "So, let me make sure I am understanding you correctly. . . . Are you saying . . . ?"
- "Could you elaborate on that point so I can fully understand what you are saying?"
- "Can you explain how you arrived at your conclusion?"
- "How do you think someone in disagreement with your point might try to argue against you?"

My colleague Justine Thanas uses a Google Chrome extension called Mote in her Social Studies classroom to provide audio recordings for student feedback. Mote's motto is "type less, talk more." Depending on the preferences of you and your students, Mote can open new lines of meaningful communication. "The students liked hearing the feedback, but there is one downfall to the recordings," admitted Thanas. "I found that if I want to go back and check what feedback I gave a student on an assignment, I had to listen to all my recordings again" (2021). As a result, Thanas uses Mote as a means for providing formative feedback on projects or shorter assignments and asks students to respond in writing by summarizing her verbal comments or replying to them directly.

Providing targeted feedback does not have to take over your life. Keep it short. The student receiving feedback should have to work harder than you do. Your feedback alone is not enough; require students to engage with your pointed comments and you will begin to see the results. Building a classroom culture that values mistakes and risk-taking will open up more opportunities to deliver honest feedback. Remember, your feedback is not the same thing as a grade.

PRINCIPLES

Incorporating effective practice means being able to identify your priorities. As teachers, there is never enough time. Be selective. Identify what your students need to improve upon to be successful on your summative assessments. If a skill isn't going to be a priority on a well-designed assessment, it's probably not worth taking the time to practice it.

Make the Time for In-Class Practice

Misconceptions take on the shortest life span when they are corrected as soon as possible. That is why in-class practice is so important for students. Trust the benefit of your presence; your feedback will be worth the class time and make a powerful impact on learning. Even short practice sessions make a big difference.

Space It Out

Design time for small and regular sessions rather than dedicating an entire period to practice. Research shows that multiple brief practice sessions are ideal for learning. Plan for five separate 10-minute practice sessions spaced out throughout a unit rather than one long 50-minute practice session. Just as we learned in Chapter 1 on retrieval, the neural pathways get stronger the more you have to go back and search for a piece of information in your long-term memory.

Practice Mindfully

Sure, repetition on its own will eventually result in some level of base competency in long-term memory. But, without time for feedback and reflection, it becomes very hard for a learner to grow and improve in a meaningful way. Regular practice sessions for which you are present and students are allotted opportunities for peer feedback will nudge them toward mindful and intentional learning.

SMALL TEACHING QUICK TIPS: PRACTICE

I know I have been adamant about the importance of allowing time for students to practice in your class and receive feedback, but this small teaching technique predominantly relies on the time you spend outside of class analyzing and strengthening your own assessments. Establish the skills your students need to be successful on your summative assessments and then provide a few little practice sessions before the big day.

· Create a timeline for yourself by prioritizing the cognitive skills students will need early in the year to be successful on your assessments. Opportunities for practice and application should directly mirror the style of your assessments.
· Review your unit plan and decide when the most appropriate times for short practice sessions will fall; indicate those dates on your syllabus so students understand their importance or make them a regular part of your weekly routine.
· Before any major assessment, stick to your practice plan. Even confident presenters will benefit from creating a main idea

slide and a script to keep them on track. Provide students with specific feedback that they have to actively engage with in some way.

CONCLUSION

The impact of practice hit me hard in my teens when I had a long stint as a summer camp counselor. It was an interesting time to work at an old-fashioned sleep-away camp with canoes and cabins because even the youngest campers were becoming increasingly reliant on mobile phones and other emerging technology. Camp offered no cellular service and nary a wi-fi network. We tried to curate a range of tech-free experiences for kids who were used to being plopped in front of a television or an iPad all day long.

On Monday mornings, we would load up the bus in the gritty industrial city where I grew up. The kids would turn up their noses at my attempts to start a sing-a-long and at my tall tales about the camp's resident mermaid as we carted them out to farm country.

"But, are there seriously no video games?" they would plead.

"Seriously," I told them.

By Saturday, the same boys who had balked at getting their sneakers dirty on the first day of camp would be sticky with bug juice and covered in face paint. We had to bribe them with ice cream sandwiches to convince them to get out of their bunks and pack up their things. They would cry big fat tears because they didn't want to go home. It's amazing how consistency and routine over the course of just one week can transform a little human into someone new.

I gained a lot of muscle memory working at camp. My hands learned to French braid, light campfires, and catch frogs without having to think twice. I'd watch rookie staff members build up a bottleneck, 30 kids deep, as they struggled to start the box stitch on the porch of the arts and crafts building. Meanwhile, my fingers could get a lanyard stitch going in mere seconds. There was never a line when I was on box stitch duty. I can still out box stitch anyone.

How did I become an arts and crafts wizard? It wasn't about my love of weaving strands of plastic string together at record pace. It was about providing kids with new and meaningful experiences.

The more complex the task, the more practice is required. Malcolm Gladwell famously popularized the 10,000-hour rule, which elaborated on research conducted in the 1970s by psychologists Herbert Simon and William Chase (Gladwell, 2013). Simon and Chase estimated a chess player would require between 10,000 and 50,000 hours of practice before becoming a Grandmaster. In his book *Outliers,* Gladwell references Microsoft co-founder Bill Gates as a prime example of the 10,000-hour rule, estimating that Gates spent 10,000 hours programming, beginning in his early teens (2008). I should note that many critics objected to the idea that Gates' success was a result of practice alone. They pointed to Gates's privilege—his mother traveled in the same circles as IBM CEO John Opel. No doubt, it took more than practice for Gates to reach such great heights; nevertheless, repetition, failure, and tenacity played important roles. Privileged or not, little Billy loved nothing more than to practice.

Some quick calculations would indicate that I have started approximately 10,000 box stitch lanyards in my lifetime. That does not equate to 10,000 hours of practice, but it's still a monumental amount of time spent on such an insignificant task. Again, I was not braiding plastic strings for my own enjoyment. I did it for the kids. Like Gates, the intrinsic motivation to practice was linked to something larger than the task itself. To watch a group of video game–obsessed 10-year-olds quietly lost in a mindful moment with their lanyards was my reward. It's no small wonder I went on to become a teacher.

I believe this is an important distinction. You can practice anything to death, but unless you draw some sort of intrinsic value from the task, it will be difficult to master. I always advise my students to figure out what feels like arduous work to most people but brings them great pleasure.

"Practice that thing continually and then charge top dollar to the people who don't want to do it themselves," I tell them.

For instance, I love to write, but many people find it torturous. At this very moment, my family is sitting on the beach lamenting the fact that I have to work during our vacation. Conversely, I am tapping away on my laptop in a Provincetown Cafe overlooking the ocean and I'm not sure I could be happier. I feel lucky to follow my passion, and as a result, I truly don't mind practicing.

Practice what you love, especially if it's something that other people hate, and you will reap the benefits.

Chapter 7

Mapping

The most effective teachers know how to create a course map that is relevant, rigorous, and manageable. It took me a long time to realize the importance of that last one. Manageability means being agile and balanced to address the needs of students while also covering the material expected of you.

A few years ago, I shared a student-teacher with another member of the English department. He was in the early stages of his practicum and spent most of his time observing us from the back of our respective classes. One day, after a morning of bouncing between our two rooms, he turned to me and said, "It's as if you are driving a racecar and she is paddling a boat."

"What does that mean?" I asked him.

According to our eager protégé, my classroom routine exhibited a high level of anticipation and control, while hers was more flexible and meandering.

"One isn't better than the other," he told me. "They're just—different."

At first, I took great pride in this comparison. In my mind, I had the command of female race car driver Danica Patrick and my colleague had a rowboat with no breaks. I doubled down on keeping a tight activity sequence and maximizing time on learning to the millisecond.

If you entered my classroom on any given day of the year, there would be three guarantees. First, students were greeted with a six-minute independent do now activity and began working immediately with no need for explanation. Next, a learning goal would be posted on the board in "kid-friendly" language and I would read it aloud to the class. Finally, an agenda always remained visible for the duration of the day, allowing students to make a mental check of our to-do list.

As Danica Patrick well knows, this level of rigid regulation occasionally leaves you with no choice but to hit the wall. An objective not met. A task on the agenda left incomplete. An activity that made perfect sense in the lesson plan and, as it turns out, sounds like utter nonsense to a bunch of 13-year-olds. Every time my habitual patterns were thrown out of whack, I became unrelenting. I felt like a total failure if things didn't go according to plan. I would go home and cry, afraid that I had failed my students in some way.

Meanwhile, my neighbor kept paddling along, slow and steady. Our class raced through twice the material, while her class paused frequently to admire the view and dig deep. I lacked her patience and profundity. She lacked my discipline and breadth.

The student-teacher had been correct in his assessment that both styles held merit. I kept circling the racetrack and trying to learn how to navigate obstacles more fluidly whenever they threatened to disrupt my routine. My journey as an educator was not without collisions, but I became increasingly efficient and so did my students. I found ways to foster student ownership within the confines of my classroom structure, and in doing so, I saw an increase in both growth and academic achievement. The most difficult adjustment for me was learning to be more flexible.

This chapter outlines conditions for nurturing an environment where deep learning can take place in a manner that intentionally requires minimal preparation or additional grading.

Employing the objectives and agendas described here will keep you on track and help your students find their balance. Just remember, even Danica makes pit stops. If I learned one thing from my colleague, it was to slow down and adjust students' practice so as not to crash and burn. Breezing through the basics to get to the "good stuff" comes with great sacrifice. My best advice is to cut yourself some slack and think about what will be most advantageous for the kids in front of you. Also, invest the time to make a detailed syllabus over the summer, and you will reap the benefits all year long. The syllabus is as much a map for you as it is for your students.

WHAT'S THE THEORY?

Mapping student learning to maximize time is a key component of any *Small Teaching* classroom. At the start of my career, I thought my daily agendas should be steadfast and unchanging. It turned out that the most important part of activating student learning was not checking everything off the list—it was establishing a strong learning goal. How we got there could differ from learner to learner. In other words, it did not so much matter how they arrived at the goal just as long as they understood their aim from the get-go.

I would like to acknowledge that while most educator evaluation rubrics require teachers to post their objectives at the start of every lesson, it's not enough to simply write a learning goal on the board. Doing an internet search for "learning objective" and then copying and pasting it to the top of your lesson plan does no one any good. The internet is a vast resource for teaching materials, but many of them are not vetted and do not encourage higher-order thinking. Stefanie Livers of Missouri State University and Victoria Miller Bennett of The Collaborative for Teaching and Learning, Louisville, have developed a protocol to help educators avoid falling into the trap of downloading cute materials that lack substance (2021). Livers and Bennett pose questions such as:

- Is it aligned with standards? If not, can it be modified so it's on target?
- What is the understanding being developed? Or is it just a following-directions task?
- Is it high-quality, promoting reasoning and problem solving?
- Does it offer an accessible, equitable opportunity for all students?
- Does it meet the preceding criteria listed?
- Does it ask students to demonstrate evidence of their thinking?

It can be very tempting to snatch up a lesson from Teachers Pay Teachers as a planning shortcut. The hard truth is, sometimes these unvetted resources do more harm than good. Make a habit of writing your own objectives according to the goal you are actually aiming for, and you will save time in the long run. Most importantly, share your objective with the kids. Articulating an objective at the start of class is one of the most concrete ways a K–8 educator can activate targeted learning. The objective explicitly tells students what they are working toward, enabling them to take risks along the way.

Writing strong objectives and making the goal or purpose of a lesson clear is particularly important for English language learners. The Sheltered Instruction Observation Protocol (SIOP) is widely used to meet needs of English language learners across America. Beyond content objectives, SIOP lesson plans include language objectives to share with students. For example, a content objective for a primary science class might state, "Students will be able to sort ten animals based on whether they are diurnal or nocturnal." The corresponding language objective would state, "Students will be able to discuss the differences between animals that are active in the daytime and animals that are active in the nighttime." Additionally, the lesson plan would stipulate key vocabulary for the science class such as: nocturnal, diurnal, nighttime, daytime, and habitat. SIOP ensures that the academic needs of English language learners are being met.

Sharing clear objectives with all students can improve learning outcomes and test scores. A meta-analysis conducted by researchers Charles Igel, Trudy Clemons, and Helen Apthorp in 2010 found an average gain of approximately 12 percentage points for learners exposed to objective setting during a lesson. "In other words, a perfectly average student—scoring at the 50th percentile on academic achievement measures—who had been exposed to objective setting strategies would be expected to perform at the 62nd percentile" (Igel et al., 2010). Evidently, when our expectations are not a guessing game, students are more likely to meet them.

To activate learning, we must provide a proverbial road map. In the classroom, this often comes in the form of an agenda or to-do list for students to follow along with. An agenda dictates a clear path toward achieving one's learning objective. The agenda lays out a plan for both my students and me to remain organized, manage our time wisely, and think ahead. Agendas and checklists are quite common in many of the workforce's most demanding fields. Pilots, surgeons, architects, and astronauts rely on checklists every day, not to avoid errors of ignorance, but rather, errors of ineptitude (Gawande, p. 8, 2009).

In his book, *The Checklist Manifesto*, surgeon and public health leader Atul Gawande encourages expert practitioners to utilize checklists as a means for slowing down (2009). He points out that we are much more forgiving when it comes to errors of ignorance than we are of ineptitude. Highly skilled, highly trained, hard-working people in the modern workplace are expected to do extraordinary things. As a result, avoidable failures persist. "And the reason is increasingly evident," writes Gawande. "The volume and complexity of what we know has exceeded our individual ability to deliver its benefit correctly, safely, or reliably. Knowledge has both saved us and burdened us" (Gawande, p. 13, 2009). That is why he proposes a simple strategy—the checklist.

The same is true of teaching. We now have access to enough reliable research on the science of learning that "best practice" actually means something. Nevertheless, wielding the tools in our toolbelt when Carissa is pocketing her seatmate's lunch money and Eddie is delivering an impromptu yodeling performance can set us off our game. Hang your checklist, typically referred to as an agenda, where everyone can see it. Gawande found that surgeons hesitant to embrace checklists were easily swayed when consulted about their own processes. Surgeons changed their attitudes when they were told something like, "We see you have a lot of experience doing this kind of surgery and we really want to understand what makes you so successful. Could you break down your process into a checklist to help us understand?" You can do the same with your students—let them take ownership of the checklist. If there are two activities on the agenda and it doesn't matter which one they do first, allow them to make the decision about what order you complete the items on your agenda. Tell them you care about their input and you want to know what order makes the most sense according to them.

Checklists and agendas also contribute positively to the social and emotional needs of our students. In recent years, educators have come to understand that leaving children metaphorically in the dark is particularly harmful to survivors of trauma. Trauma can refer to abuse or neglect, but it is also relevant to the collective experience of a large-scale tragedy like the COVID-19 pandemic. Heather C. Forkey, MD, is the clinical director of the

Foster Children Evaluation Service and chief of the Division of Child Protection for the UMass Memorial Children's Medical Center. Her work emphasizes the importance of establishing routines for educators and other youth workers. "Routines really shut down the stress response," explained Forkey. "Most people can remember the end of March 2020; with everything out of routine, you spent the day spinning and thinking, 'I should be doing something. I know there's something I should be doing, but I can't do it and I can't think.' That was the impact of stress hormones hitting a part of our brain called the prefrontal cortex, which is responsible for keeping us organized and focused." Forkey's research shows that teachers who institute dependable routines are able to calm the prefrontal cortex for their students and shut down the stress response, sometimes before it starts. She is especially passionate about the practice of making charts, such as agendas, for students who are prone to a fight-or-flight response when they are triggered during the course of the school day.

One of the easiest ways to alleviate a student's anxiety is to create a secure and predictable environment from the moment they walk into the classroom. Providing a "bell-ringer" or "do now" activity that requires no introduction or explanation and appears in the same location every day will set the foundation for learning. The activity should be designed to preview the day's lesson or draw on the previous day's lesson. Ideally, it takes five or six minutes and allows the teacher an opportunity to take attendance and complete other daily "administrivia" without detracting from time spent on learning. I like to display a timer so students have a precise measure of how long the first step on our agenda will take.

As Benedict Carey puts it in his book *How We Learn*, "Having a goal foremost in mind tunes our perceptions to fulfilling it. And that tuning determines, to some extent, where we look and what we notice" (2014a, p. 140). For example, if you are hiking on an unfamiliar mountain trail marked with blue triangles, you will begin filtering every step through two distinct filters: "Am I on the trail?" and "Can I see a blue triangle up ahead?" When you get to the summit, you will probably be capable of recalling your general route, but unlikely to describe the layout of the mountain and answer questions like: "How many other hikers did you pass?" or "What direction was the stream flowing?" Your sense of purpose was focused on following the blue triangles to achieve a specific goal. Explicitly sharing our goals and learning objectives creates a strong sense of purpose for our students. By telling students exactly what we want them to learn, we heighten their attention and direct them toward productivity.

Drawing clear attention to long-term or overarching learning goals is equally important. Like the hiker on the mountain who notices the blue triangles, a student familiar with the title of your unit will be more likely to zero in on significant themes that appear again and again throughout your lessons. Instructional coach Harvey Silver recommends adding "a study in . . ." or "a study of . . ." to the title of every unit (McTighe, 2016). This small change can help bring a unit of study into focus for students. He shares the following examples:

· A unit on the rainforest – A study of a complex ecosystem
· A unit on decimals, fractions, and percentages – A study of equivalence
· A unit on the story "Frog and Toad Are Friends" – A study of true friendship
· A unit on World War I – A study of unintended consequences
· A unit on weight training – A study of proper technique

The fewer secrets we keep from our students, the better. Be clear about exactly what you would like them to take away from your lesson and they will be much more likely to do so.

Stating the objective, sharing an agenda, and starting class with a consistent routine every day will propel learning outcomes for your students and provide them with a map for success. Routines provide a sense of safety and security for even the most timid learners in addition to reducing teacher planning time by replicating successful structures again and again.

IN SHORT

· Your learning goal should be clearly established at the opening and closing of your lesson.
· It is perfectly acceptable for different learners to arrive at your learning goal in different ways.
· The internet is a vast resource for learning objectives and lesson plans, but many of them are not vetted and do not encourage higher-order thinking.
· Posting an agenda or checklist for students to refer to throughout the lesson can help ease their anxieties and keep you on target.
· Following a predictable routine is especially helpful for survivors of trauma.
· Telling students what we want them to learn makes them more attentive and productive.
· Bring your objectives into focus by adding "a study in" or "a study of . . ." to the title of your unit.

MODELS

As humans, we generally prefer to take the shortest path to any difficult task. I mean this quite literally. One New York-based marketing firm, Dstillery, tracked 7.5 million mobile devices over the course of a month, only to find that a longer commute to the gym was associated with fewer visits (Bachman, 2017). According to the study, "People who go to the gym once a month travel a median distance of 5.1 miles. Those who go five or more times a month travel 3.7 miles" (Bachman, 2017). The same is true of our students. The more obstacles they must overcome to arrive at a learning outcome, the less likely they are to make an attempt. Make it easy for them. Map a direct route to your goal.

Mapping learning with a steadfast routine will likely require more discipline from you than it does from your students. *Small Teaching* can help you set the guidelines for success by maximizing class time with bite-sized components. Trust that even the most challenging students will be grateful for a sense of consistency at the start of class and begin to meet your rigorous expectations more readily.

Year-Long Theme

"Miss, why are we doing this?"

Like all of us, students don't want to waste their time on irrelevant course material. They want to know how it connects to the big picture.

Pick a year-long theme or an overarching goal for your entire course. Having a clear purpose, particularly one that relates your content area to the outside world, will make your lessons feel more relevant. Post your year-long theme prominently in your classroom. Write it on every assignment. Put it at the top of your syllabus.

To save myself the stress of fumbling for an answer about why we are analyzing text structure or interpreting the meaning of an author's word choice, I make sure to pick a broad enough theme that I can connect it to everything we do all year long.

The concept of defining an overarching goal or year-long theme comes from the seminal work of Grant Wiggins and Jay McTighe, *Understanding by Design*, which outlines a framework for course development called "Backward Design" (2005). Wiggins and McTighe urge educators to begin with their end goal. Don't ask students to build a replica of a covered wagon because you think the project will result in cute displays for your classroom. Instead, ask them to build a covered wagon because they are exploring your year-long theme of "perseverance."

Think of your activity as the smallest nesting doll within a much larger framework. The activity lives inside of your learning objective, which is contained by a unit of study. On the outermost layer is a year-long theme. A year-long theme could be something as general as "change," "civic engagement," or "relationships."

As a middle school English teacher, I have selected year-long themes such as: justice, equality, kindness, and community to guide my classes in the past. I make sure the theme I pick is broad enough in scope that I can clearly connect our daily objectives back to it without any trouble. When the book *Wonder* by R. J. Palacio became popular nearly a decade ago, my students began referring to our theme as a "precept."

In the novel, a teacher named Mr. Browne declares a new theme to guide his class every month. In 2016, Palacio published a spin-off titled *365 Days of Wonder: Mr. Browne's Book of Precepts*, which I have found to be an excellent resource for educators in search of year-long themes to guide their coursework.

One of my former colleagues, Wendy Walsh, is now the social emotional program director at a suburban Massachusetts middle school. This year, her principal asked staff to focus on the overarching theme of "resilience." He got their attention by renaming the decades old teams (the cohorts of students who share the same core teachers) to emphasize his goal. Previously, the teams had all been named for gems—Pearl, Ruby, Emerald, Sapphire, Diamond, and Onyx.

"Now, the sixth-grade teams are Sharks and Stingrays— creatures that swim," explained Walsh. "Seventh are Lemurs and Polar bears—creatures that walk or climb, and eighth grade teams are Dragons and Phoenixes—creatures that fly" (Walsh, 2021). The creatures were meant to represent the developmental stages of middle school students. For her own year-long theme, Walsh selected a corresponding quote from Dr. Martin Luther King Jr.: "If you can't fly then run, if you can't run then walk, if you can't walk then crawl, but whatever you do you have to keep moving forward." She hopes to encapsulate the school-wide theme in her own classroom by pointing students back to the quote with each new unit of study.

Walsh appreciates the relevant and applicable nature of her principal's focus on resilience. "I think it's broad enough to reach staff and students in multiple contexts," said Walsh. "In my new role as a social emotional program director, the content I cover runs the gamut, but the idea of continuing to move forward fits a variety of situations, whether it's working through a complex math equation, returning to school after a hospitalization, or recovering from a traumatic event" (2021). Goodness knows, we all have our own trauma to process in the aftermath of the pandemic. Choosing a singular theme at least gets us on the same page.

Year-Long Theme: Perseverance

"We can push ourselves further. We always have more to give."
Simone Biles

1st Quarter

Guiding Questions:
How is society shaped and shifted by injustice?
How do both persuasive and suspenseful forms of writing and speaking affect the reader or listener emotionally?

Possible Materials:
"One Million Volumes" by Rudolfo Anaya
"Because of Libraries" by Naomi Shihab Nye
"The Lady, or the Tiger" by Frank R. Stockton
"The Dinner Party" by Mona Gardner

Assessments:
Daily Journal
Debate
Persuasive Composition
(with a thesis)

Foundational Skills:
Metaphors & Symbols
Mood & Tone
Persuasive Appeals

2nd Quarter

Guiding Questions:
How have words helped us to overcome great obstacles throughout history?
Why is it important to record one's thoughts and feelings in times of great injustice?
What effect does prejudice have on the powers of persuasion?

Possible Materials:
Excerpts from "All But My Life" & "A Diary from Another World" by Gerda Weissmann Klein
"Todesfuge" by Paul Celan
Universal Declaration of Human Rights
Facing History & Ourselves:
Current Events

Assessments:
Daily Journal
RAFT Project

Foundational Skills:
Activating Prior Knowledge
Establishing a Position
Rhetorical Analysis

3rd Quarter	4th Quarter
Guiding Questions:	*Guiding Questions:*
How do activists employ the power of persuasive language?	*How has our nation transformed over time with the growth of communication?*
How do issues of racism permeate the language of our current society?	*How does social media aid or hinder clear communication?*
What makes a source reputable?	
Possible Materials:	Possible Materials:
"Harriet Tubman"	Literature Circle Selections:
by Ann Petry	*I am Malala* by
Nikki Giovanni	Malala Yousafzai
Langston Hughes	*Fat Chance, Charlie Vega* by
Emmett Till	Crystal Maldonado
Busing Boston	*This is Where it Ends* by
	Marieke Nijkamp
Assessments:	*Stamped* by Jason Reynolds and
Daily Journal	Ibram X. Kendi
Debate	*Hey, Kiddo* by Jarrett
Research Thesis	J. Krosoczka
Foundational Skills:	Assessments:
Summarizing vs. Paraphrasing	Daily Journal
Repetition	Social Media Project
Compare and Contrast	Lit Circles
Using Literary Elements and Techniques	
	Foundational Skills:
	Style Analytics
	Analyzing Argument
	Levels of Questioning

Writing an Objective

You've seen it before. Uncle Bill loudly proclaims on his Facebook feed, "I am going to lose 10 pounds this month!" Why is he sharing this personal goal with the world? To hold himself accountable. Much like the emotional stakes of making a public prediction discussed in Chapter 3, stating a goal or objective publicly comes with a certain sense of obligation. Uncle Bill's goal sounds like a decent one. It's measurable. It's obviously important enough to him that he put it out there for everyone to see. Uncle Bill seems dead set on devising an appropriate plan to achieve his weight-loss goal, perhaps with the input of his followers. I wish him well.

Like Uncle Bill, you must work backward in your daily planning for students to gain a clear understanding of what they are expected to achieve. Lessons that help students access the highest levels of thinking are not dependent on flashy activities. Don't get me wrong, new and empowering experiences are terrific, but that comes after you decide on a learning objective for the class. Remember, it's okay if different learners arrive at your goal in different ways.

In his technique-driven guide, *Teach Like a Champion*, school leadership consultant Doug Lemov lays out four simple criteria for writing a strong objective, which they call "the 4 Ms" (2010).

- The objective must be **manageable**, meaning it can be mastered during a single lesson.
- It must be **measurable** so both you and your students can gauge at the end of the lesson whether or not you achieved it.
- The objective must be **made first**—in other words, it comes before you decide on the activities.
- It should be **most important**—a pivotal takeaway from the lesson that directly correlates with your state or Common Core Standards.

A poor objective might be something as vague and unmeasurable as: "Students will be able to know elements from the periodic table." An objective that follows the 4 Ms would be far more specific, stating something like: "Students will be able to compare a metal, a nonmetal, and a metalloid based on their properties and their locations in the periodic table."

Lemov places far greater value on attaining the objective than executing a mind-bogglingly complicated activity to impress your principal. "Opt for the most direct route from point to point, the Shortest Path to the goal. Eschew the complex if something less clever, less cutting-edge, less artfully constructed will yield a better result" (Lemov, 2010). Student learning is intricate enough on its own, so simplify the process by setting a clear goal in line with the 4 Ms.

Model Objective:

Measurable	Made First	Most Important	Manageable
✓	✓	✓	✓

Students will be able to form original predictions about the end of the story using at least three pieces of textual evidence to support their ideas.

Write your objective below.

Measurable	Made First	Most Important	Manageable

Bloom's Taxonomy Word Bank:

Level of Thinking	Useful Verbs
Remember	Recall, Define, Identify
Understand	Summarize, Paraphrase, Explain
Apply	Select, Act Out, Build
Analyze	Compare, Contrast, Examine
Evaluate	Debate, Judge, Recommend
Create	Imagine, Pretend, Design

Post an Agenda

Students want to feel secure in your classroom at all times. To build a safe environment in which they can take risks, it is important to keep them abreast of the day's activities. Not only will referencing an agenda throughout class help ease anxiety, but it will also help students slot new information into the context of your learning objective.

Check items off the list as you accomplish them. A great agenda will account for every moment of class time to maximize learning. Start with a bell-ringer or do now as an easy way to decrease transition times for intermediate and middle school grades where switching classes is common practice. Even the lower elementary grades have to navigate transition times. Returning from recess or lunch is the perfect opportunity to reinforce routines for younger elementary students.

After the do now is complete, review your objective, introduce a mini-lesson, and then dive into application. Always end with an exit ticket to help gauge whether or not your students achieved their goal for the day.

A typical agenda in my classroom looks like this:

1. Do Now
2. Mini-Lesson: "The Aha! Moment"
3. Literature Circle Read Aloud Ch. 5
4. Compose "Aha!" Statements
5. Share Out
6. Exit Ticket

Agendas and checklists save lives every day in operating rooms across America. I can't promise yours will do the same but posting a detailed agenda will certainly keep you on target to help students achieve your goal. Even the most expert veteran teachers can inadvertently forget an important step here or there, especially if they've had to teach the same lesson five periods in a row. Give yourself the gift of a concrete agenda and the satisfaction of checking off items.

PRINCIPLES

The more efficiently you use your class time, the less work you and your students will have to do outside of the school day. A *Small Teaching* approach to mapping means being consistent in your routines, and flexible in your thinking. The following principles can help activate learning in your classroom from the moment students step foot through the door.

Set a Timer

Remember that every second you have with your students is precious. Setting a timer for the start of class activities not only encourages students to get right to work, it also shows students that you value their time. Let the timer dictate the tone. Students might feel rushed at first, but they will develop a better sense of time management before they know it. My students enjoy the Mr. Timer YouTube channel, which offers over 100 intervals and themes for students to choose from.

Utilize Strong Verbs

In Part I of this book, I discuss Bloom's Taxonomy as a structural template for deep learning to occur. As you write your objectives, it is important to return to the Taxonomy and draw on some of the strong verbs associated with all six levels of thinking. Your objective will not fall in the highest tiers of Bloom's Taxonomy every single day. That would be like skipping the lower rungs of a ladder and falling flat on your face. Consider verbs at (1) Remembering: list, define, recall; (2) Understanding: summarize, paraphrase, explain; (3) Applying: build, choose, solve; (4) Analyzing: compare, contrast, survey; (5) Evaluating: debate, recommend, disprove; and (6) Creating: imagine, propose, and invent.

Objective Exemplars:

1. Remembering: Students will be able to identify the rising action, climax, and falling action on a plot diagram.
2. Understanding: Students will be able to explain the difference between a state and a country by writing a short paragraph that includes a thesis statement.
3. Applying: Students will be able to correctly solve at least three out of five trigonometry problems using the formulas provided.
4. Analyzing: Students will be able to categorize cell parts with a graphic organizer after reading an article about the differences between plant and animal cells.
5. Evaluating: Students will be able to defend the actions of a wartime president in a formal class debate.

6. Creating: Students will be able to form original predictions about the end of the story using at least three pieces of textual evidence to support their ideas.

Don't Be Afraid to Dipstick

Take a casual peek to see how full the tank is. Make it quick. I do not grade bell-ringers or do nows. When the timer goes off, I ask a small handful of students to share and it provides me with a baseline understanding of their prior knowledge. Google Classroom's "Question" feature is my favorite means for assigning a bell-ringer. You can choose whether or not you want students to see one another's answers and get a good sense of a class's entry point just by quickly skimming through the answers yourself. This is an example of a low-stakes "dipstick" to help you gauge the big picture progress happening in your classroom. Do not feel guilty for collecting sample sets on a regular basis for your own planning benefits. Not every assignment warrants lengthy individualized feedback.

SMALL TEACHING QUICK TIPS: MAPPING

It's simple—the more defined your routine becomes, the more learning can take place. The most crucial routine comes at the very beginning. Set the stage for student success during the first 10 minutes of a lesson by providing a bell-ringer, articulating a clear and achievable goal, and sharing your agenda.

· Determine a year-long theme. Make sure it is broad enough that it can be applied to every unit of study throughout the year. (Example: Perseverance, Citizenship, Respect.)
· Write your objectives first. Figure out the overarching goal of your lesson before you settle on the engaging activities that will

get you there. Objectives should follow Doug Lemov's 4 Ms: manageable, measurable, made first, and most important.

· Posting an agenda for the duration of class will help you cultivate a trauma-informed classroom and it will ultimately help all of your students to master the objective you set for them. You might not get to everything on your agenda and that's okay. If you don't complete an item on your list, it's important to adjust and try to figure out the shortest path to your objective.

CONCLUSION

The most innovative course map I have ever seen in a classroom came from Clark University marketing professor Lawrence Norman who spent more than two decades building the Adidas brand. Norman's course is highly structured, adhering to a strict syllabus. Despite the constraints of firm due dates and reading assignments, Norman manages to stay extraordinarily current by creating a "playlist" for every class meeting in lieu of a traditional agenda. The playlist consists of relevant video clips, memes, and songs to accompany each agenda item.

"Whatever is in the news that week, or even that day, on top of any appropriate business topics will always dictate the playlist," he explained (2021). Norman strikes a fine balance between maintaining authority, staying on target, and imbuing relevance into his instructional style. He does not have an ancient binder in his desk drawer to determine what students will do on any given day, simply because it was what they did last year and the year before that. Instead, he takes the skeleton of a lesson and fleshes it out with contemporary culture. His students are happy to provide recommendations.

Norman's ability to channel balance and flexibility comes from a defined sense of purpose. He began working for Adidas in

Israel while he was playing professional basketball in the late 1990s. "I would take three buses to work at 6:00 in the morning, work from 7 a.m. to 7 p.m., then take three buses to night practice from 8:00 p.m. to 10:30 p.m., and then take three buses to get home by midnight," recalled Norman (2021). He maintained this demanding schedule for three and a half years, learning to willfully budget his time. Norman went on to become the head of business and brand affairs, the right-hand strategy man to the CEO of Adidas. Before long, he was named the global head of basketball. Norman worked closely with NBA point guard Derrick Rose on a tremendously popular campaign called "The Return."

Observing Norman's class at Clark is like watching a complex series of plays unfold on the basketball court. His playlist helps students stay oriented and commands their curiosity with music and other relevant media.

Norman's class "Marketing to You" has grown increasingly popular at Clark because his overarching goal is made clear in every lesson, every assignment, and every exam. "I prepare students to step in and contribute to global brands and startups on day one," he said. Norman emphasizes this goal again and again, reminding students that great brands need them. "Companies outsource to external agencies to acquire the knowledge and skill sets needed to best target and reach people like my students," he explained "Wouldn't it be better to go straight to the source and hire them straight out of college?" (2021).

In order to help students value their own skill sets, Norman integrates familiar music and pop culture into his daily playlist. Students are able to formulate connections between their overarching course goal of "contributing to global brands" and their existing passions or interests. It's okay to be iron-fisted about your year-long theme or the objectives that guide your lessons. But, be flexible in how you arrive at that theme or achieve those objectives. Norman's course content remains steady, but the delivery method changes based on the students he has in front of him. Most of all, he manages his time well and redirects every activity back to the overarching course goal.

Mapping the learning process from the moment students step foot in your classroom is crucial to maximizing your time and theirs. Remember, research shows that by setting clear goals and laying out the steps to achieve those objectives, your students will be approximately 12% more likely to make gains (Igel, 2010). The younger the student, the more important the routine. Students who learn to be productive during the school day will be more prepared to transfer those skills to independent environments. Try to be realistic in your goal setting, and don't panic if you find your agenda needs adjustments. If you know where you are going, it will be much easier to arrive there safely.

The Playlist Craft your agenda like an album or a playlist.

Include links to relevant and appropriate music, memes, and news stories.

Example:

Album Title	**"Sour"**	**Year-Long Theme: Perseverance**
Artist	By Olivia Rodrigo	English Language Arts
Track 1	1. brutal *"I don't even know where to start . . ."* ♪	Do Now
Track 2	2. traitor *"All the questions you used to avoid . . ."* ♪	Turn-and-Talk
Track 3	3. drivers license *"I still hear your voice . . ."* ♪	Read Aloud

Album Title	"Sour"	Year-Long Theme: Perseverance
Track 4	4. 1 step forward, 3 steps back *"It's back and forth, goin' over everything I said"* ♪	Three-Two-One
Track 5	5. deja vu *"But it's all reused ..."* ♪	Review
Track 6	6. good 4 u *"You look happy and healthy ..."* ♪	Exit Ticket

How does each activity on our agenda relate to the corresponding Olivia Rodrigo song?

The Playlist Craft your agenda like an album or a playlist.

Include links to relevant and appropriate music, memes, and news stories.

Album Title	Year-Long Theme:
Artist	Subject:
Track 1	
Track 2	
Track 3	
Track 4	
Track 5	
Track 6	

How does each activity on our agenda relate to the corresponding song?

Chapter 8

Putting It All Together: Jennessa Burks, Grade 4 Teacher

Jennessa Burks is a fourth-grade teacher in Cambridge, Massachusetts. Burks fosters higher level thinking among her elementary students by helping them recognize connections, form their own predictions, and synthesize new material. You will find her total embrace of growth mindset language is an excellent introduction to Chapter 9, which is dedicated entirely to "Growing."

How do you encourage students to discuss their strengths and weaknesses with one another?

I think this one gets a little bit tricky for me, especially if we're talking about post-pandemic learning. Right now we are verbalizing strengths and strengths only when we speak with each other. Academic weaknesses are a tough area right now. The only thing that we're talking about when it comes to addressing struggles and challenges with each other are the social emotional things that are coming out during restorative circles. That just feels like a safe time for students, but they always have the opportunity to opt out.

Can you explain what a restorative circle looks like?

Absolutely. I can't take any credit for it. This is something that's done all over the place. Restorative circles bring your class together as a community in a literal circle. You usually have a display at the center. Students start to take ownership of the circle and start to build themselves up to facilitate it. It is a tool for community building and problem solving. A talking tool gets passed around the circle and students have the agency to be able to pass or to share as much as they want. One norm that students have established in my circle this year is that "stories stay and the learning leaves." So, what we learn from each other's stories can leave our circle, but any specifics we share about our own lives are asked to respectfully stay in the circle. So far, we're having a great time. When it comes to verbalizing strengths, we praise all different qualities, academic and social. I encourage students to share their own strengths and also recognize the strengths in other students and encourage them. We've kind of banned negative language. We never say "That person is just not a science person" because that's not really true. Maybe they're not doing great at science right now. We turned the conversation to ask, "What are they doing really well at? And why?" A lot of the praise consists of comments like, "I notice that person is trying really hard and I know they've practiced a lot on their own." I think prior to the pandemic, this is something that students might have already had a grasp on without the restorative circle. But, we're noticing that things are different now because they have not necessarily practiced those skills for a year and a half. The last time my kiddos were in school was second grade and now they're in fourth. It's a big jump.

How do you implement meaningful practice in your fourth-grade classroom?

When I think of meaningful practice, I think of students having the chance to confer with each other, whether it's that they've worked independently and then they're getting a chance to share their products or if they are collaboratively working together. I also think of students being given feedback from me or from peers. I think that praise and feedback helps them make meaning of their work. I often explain the "why." We'll be practicing a task and I'll pause to say, "This is the task at hand, but let me tell you why this is gonna be important and why this is going to be helpful for you." For instance, we're working on writing narratives right now. We were talking about what we would add into an introduction to hook our reader and why it's so important to hook a reader. We read some nonexamples of stories that we just wanted to put down because they didn't capture our attention. I think nonexamples help students make meaning and understand what their practice should be focused on. They're not just doing a task, they get to see the bigger picture of why developing the skill is valuable.

And when you're giving this reinforcement and feedback, what kind of language are you using?

The more specific you can be, the better. We don't say things like, "Good job! That looks great!" Instead, we would say, "I love how you persevered through the story problem. It had multiple steps that were really challenging and you didn't give up." When students are having a difficult time with writing, I would say, "I really loved that you asked for help and then you were able to come up with five small moments to choose from because I know generating ideas can be a really difficult task." I think it's important to provide specifics for students when we give positive praise and acknowledge times when things can feel tricky. We are a heavy praise classroom. I also praise them for giving me grace. I appreciate when they help me gather my thought process. I always praise them when the day gets really hectic and they maintain their composure, or for being flexible when the school has to change our schedule. As a result, I think they're more apt to praise each other and me.

How do you create a safe environment for students to find their own voices and take risks?

I think a big part of creating a space where students can speak up and take risks is maintaining a routine of predictability. Students have to know when it's okay to talk and when it's not. They also have to learn what language to use and how to be kind to one another. If they're worried that they're going to say the wrong thing or hurt someone's feelings or get in trouble for what comes out of their mouths, then they're not going to speak. Another thing is, I think you have to model and you have to give them the space to feel comfortable enough to correct, even you. I often give examples of things that I have flubbed up with throughout the day or said wrong. I make errors intentionally in my spelling and in my calculations so that the students get practice with correcting me in polite ways. Right now, we're doing phonics in fourth grade for the first time. It's a brand-new program. We got a new curriculum and I was transparent with my students. I said, "Hey, friends, I've never taught this before. It's a very big curriculum for me to learn and there will be times that I make mistakes." And they said, "It's okay." They've been really great at rating me at the end. I got stuck one of the days and I said, "I think I need your help. How do we do this?" They said, "Miss Burks, it's a productive struggle. You can figure it out." They threw my own words back at me.

How do you teach synthesis at the elementary level?

When we're trying to teach students skills, we have to move beyond seeing those skills in isolation. If the skills that we need students to learn are making text connections, students need to be able to make connections constantly between what they are learning and real life. For me, I make a lot of connections throughout the day and we even have a hand signal to show that I'm making a connection. I use hand signals as nonverbal cues for friends all the time. We've got a little hand signal that I can do that will demonstrate there's a connection to be made with something. We make connections across the curriculum. There's a lot of science and social studies content that gets pulled into literacy, and there's some science that gets pulled into math. We make connections to stories, events, or different occurrences that have happened in our community or in our families. We welcome them, even though sometimes the conversations get a little long. I think students need to be able to practice the skill itself before they can implement it. With higher level texts the connections may not feel normalized because now we're asking them to activate many different skills at the same time. If we're not making connections on a regular basis and then we're asking them to read at a deeper level to make inferences and to synthesize as well as write a response—they are going to struggle. And we know that all those skills require different approaches and we're asking kids to merge them altogether. We have to be able to practice these skills constantly if we want our students to become synthesizers.

Part III

Transforming: Balance and Agility

At the start of every school year, our students are thrust into unfamiliar territory. The more predictable we can make a new situation or environment, the more likely our students become to embrace their own vulnerabilities and experience growth. This is where powerful learning occurs. While trying to prepare for a new crop of students, I often consider my own struggles as a college swimmer.

My high school swim team practiced every day at a crumbling community college pool. It was always too cold. There were no diving blocks. The lane lines would snag on our suits. Despite less-than-glamorous conditions, I loved to swim.

Swimming demanded my complete attention to the present, imparting an acute awareness of my own breath. I am prone to thinking my way out of uncomfortable experiences, but 5 a.m.

practices taught me the tenets of mindfulness long before Oprah or Gwyneth made it trendy. In the pool, there were no escapes or distractions, save the bold linear markers along the bottom of each lane. Under water, I allowed myself to perceive excruciating pain with sharp attention and find balance and flexibility within myself.

Swimming also gave me an affinity for storing data sets in my head. Intervals, splits, and yardage totals propelled my internal calculator. Every second of swim practice required a level of mathematical grappling I now reserve for tax season. The sport increased my endurance both physically and intellectually. There was a time in my life when I could tell you exactly how long it took for a minute to pass without counting the seconds or consulting a clock. I possessed an intimate knowledge of time. I knew what one minute felt like. Now, I admit, my brain is so nurtured by iPhone algorithms that it struggles to compute more than one thing at a time.

Back then, I lived for the euphoric feeling of touching the wall at the end of a race or a workout. There is a weightless, tingling sense of self-worth that nothing but speed can inspire. Swimming is punishing in the moment and blissful after the fact—the opposite of bourbon. It is its own reward.

During my senior year of high school, I was recruited to a Division 1 college swim program. My eyes teared up on the official visit when I saw all of the state-of-the-art equipment, electronic timing pads, and the bright clean deck. I had never been privy to such luxurious training conditions. With access to Division 1 resources, I was confident I could reach my full potential.

There were a few big differences between high school and college swimming. While my high school coach had always posted the entire workout and total yardage on the board before practice, my college coach preferred to add each set, line by line as we went through practice. My high school coach made adjustments as necessary and emphasized our focus for the day. My college coach left us in suspense. It killed me. I lost my balance and my motivation.

I found myself wasting mental energy by stressing over how much effort to expel or conserve. Was this the main set or part of the warmup? Was practice nearly over or did we have thousands of yards left to go? It wasn't the training itself that exhausted me, but the not-knowing. I craved predictability. Having an overarching goal and a clear understanding of our agenda had kept me afloat and helped me work together with my high school teammates. By contrast, secrecy left me drowning in a silo of anxiety during my college career. My times never got faster. By senior year, I was repulsed by the sticky texture of a bathing cap.

I've avoided indoor pools for a decade—abandoned gurgling basins, eluded lapping gutters, sworn off turbid deck air. The smell of chlorine still exhausts me. It's the scent of irrecoverable talent. A bouquet of fear. My experience in college left me lost, without a map. This can also be the case in our classrooms if we neglect to create balance and predictability for our students.

Chapter 9

Growing

The research of Carol Dweck, discussed at length later in this chapter, delves into the value of effort praise. Effort praise means lauding children for their hard work rather than their natural talent—"you must have worked very hard" versus "you must be very smart." At best, students should not be compared to anyone but their former selves and they should be celebrated for growth over achievement the majority of the time.

In my current position as the library media specialist at a large urban middle school, I was not expecting to teach classes. It was meant to be more of a coaching role. Until, of course, the first day of school when the new reading teacher didn't show up and the instructional technology teacher quit. Suddenly, I found myself responsible for teaching four classes in four different rooms, in addition to my responsibilities in the library. The rest of my department had felt the brunt of the staffing-shortage as well, with class sizes rising to nearly 30.

"I have to ask you for a favor," my principal told me on my second week. "I need you to teach one more class."

"Of course," I said. After all, I thought I was Hillary Swank in *Freedom Writers*. I was going to change the world.

"We'll keep your numbers low," she promised.

"Bring it on," I said.

The other technology teachers took it upon themselves to hand pick who they would siphon off and transfer into my newly created class. I didn't think much of it until our first class meeting. Somehow, I had managed to land 10 of the vice principal's regular customers. That first day was mayhem.

In over a decade of teaching, I had always counted my classroom management as a strength, but this was truly pitiful. They yelled. They roughhoused. They played obnoxious yodeling videos on YouTube that drove me insane. I maintained consistent routines. I called home. I praised them constantly. For the first two weeks, nothing seemed to work.

It didn't take long to find out more about the young men who were giving me a run for my money. Most of them lived nearby in a low-income housing project known as The Valley. One of the boys, I'll call him Eddie, spent the majority of our class time running around the room like a madman yelling, "Shuuuuut up!" with the same cadence of a screeching seagull.

The more I learned about his life outside of school, the more I felt empathetic toward him—and yet I couldn't get the sound of his voice out of my head while I lay in bed at night. "Shuuuuut up!" I heard it over and over.

I knew I needed to readjust my approach if we were going to achieve our goals for the year. Suddenly, the state test scores became the last thing on my mind. Growth meant making it through one class period without having to hear someone yodel or bray, "Shuuuuut up!" I needed to start measuring these kids against their previous selves. We all needed to get stronger together.

The next day, I posed the following question: "What is something about our city that you think could be better?"

One student raised his hand and said, "This place is trash."

"Shuuuuut up!" yelled Eddie.

"Let's hear him out," I said. "I agree, we have a real problem with trash. Maybe we could research some solutions."

"No, I mean this place is trash because there's nothing to do here," he told me. "I wish The Valley had a soccer field." Even Eddie fell quiet.

It was true, a subsequent search revealed that of the 899 apartments in The Valley, 807 contained children. We also confirmed that soccer was indeed the most popular sport across the globe, and The Valley was the most culturally diverse community in our city. From that class period, the idea for Valley Field—a safe place to bring many cultures together—was born.

We spent our time researching urban planning, scouting locations on Google Earth, budgeting for proper equipment, and identifying a feasible community partner. The kids even built a scaled model of the field and created a stop-motion video to pitch their idea. We submitted a proposal to the local housing authority and they agreed to come in for a meeting. I held my breath.

Sure, my students had grown more productive in class; however, their behavior was still maniacal most days. I lost count of the number of times I had revoked glue gun privileges from Eddie. Things were better, but still chaotic. When I asked the head principal for permission to invite our visitors into school, she agreed, but told me she would also have to be present for the meeting.

On the day of the big presentation, I was shocked to find everyone had arrived early to class. They helped me set out a tablecloth and flowers. Eddie insisted on greeting and escorting our visitors up to the room. Upon arrival, the Deputy Director of Development remarked, "What a gentleman." My eyes grew wide in disbelief.

My students took the lead, clicking through a slideshow presentation and fielding questions. In the end, the housing authority agreed to fund the whole project. There was a lot of handshaking and praise rippling throughout the room. Eddie offered to walk our guests to the door.

"I am so impressed by their maturity," the Director told me.

"Me too," I said, flabbergasted.

My head principal looked pleased as well, although she did have one question for me when everybody else had gone. "How did you end up with this particular group of high-needs students, all in one class?" she asked. "I wish you had told me so I could have provided you with the necessary support."

I should have known better than to try to be a hero. By failing to ask for help, I had let my ego get in the way of what was best for the kids.

The Valley Field project gave me more pride than perfect scores on the state test ever could. We all grew stronger that semester. My students learned to work together to make their dreams a reality, and I learned to ask my administrators for what I needed. Sometimes growth is the greatest outcome of all.

WHAT'S THE THEORY?

The seminal study on growth was published in 1998 by two Columbia University Psychologists, Claudia Mueller and Carol Dweck. Mueller and Dweck focused on praise, believing that children who were praised for natural ability or talent could face negative impacts on learning. They reasoned that by focusing on natural ability and talent, teachers were reinforcing the misconception that intelligence is unchanging. Effort praise, on the other hand, could encourage students to seek out rigor and work hard to achieve their goals.

Mueller and Dweck gave over 100 fifth graders 4 minutes to solve 10 math problems. All students were told "Wow, you did very well on these problems" (p. 36). A control group received no additional praise, while others were told either, "You must be smart at these problems" or "You must have worked hard at these problems" (p. 36). Next, the children were all given 10 more problems and told they performed "a lot worse," regardless of their achievement. When the students were given 10 more problems to solve, those who had been praised for their natural intelligence enjoyed the task less and were less likely to persist than those praised for effort (p. 37). The group praised for their intelligence decreased their performance on the final set of problems.

Dweck's fully formed theory came to be known as mindset, discussed in her aptly titled 2008 book *Mindset: The New Psychology of Success*. Dweck divided learners into two groups: fixed mindset and growth mindset. Individuals with a fixed mindset believed their intelligence was predetermined and their potential was limited. Simply put, students with a fixed mindset believed they could not succeed in school because they were not intelligent enough. By contrast, individuals with a growth mindset recognized their limitations, but believed their intelligence could improve throughout their lives with hard work.

I find math and English to be the most divisive subjects. I, myself, have been known to tell people I'm "not a math person." I try to remember to say, "I have to work very hard at math, but it feels so good when I am successful" when I'm in the earshot of students. It is possible to not be very good at something right now, but that does not bar you from becoming a talented mathematician in the future. We can make ourselves smarter through hard work. This is not to say our potential is unlimited. There is a spectrum in which we all fall; however, we are not stuck in one position on the intelligence spectrum. Dweck writes, "Scientists are learning that people have more capacity for lifelong learning and brain development than they ever thought. Of course, each person has a unique genetic endowment. People may start with different temperament and different aptitudes, but it is clear that experience, training, and personal effort take them the rest of the way" (p. 5). Dweck found that intelligence was not the only thing that could grow and change. One's mindset could change, too.

Mindset can intersect with grit. In 2017, I had the opportunity to attend the ASU+GSV Summit keynote delivered in San Diego by preeminent scholar on grit, Angela Duckworth. She rocked my worldview. Duckworth began her career as a teacher before becoming a psychologist and authoring the *New York Times* best-selling book *Grit: The Power of Passion and Perseverance*. In her research, she found that self-control and perseverance were not enough to account for grit. Exceptionalism requires passion. Duckworth describes passion as the drive to stay consistent or loyal to something over a long period of time (2016, p. 8). Beyond a strong interest in one's craft, she observed that gritty people were willing to practice with intention, find purpose beyond themselves, and maintain a sense of hopefulness in the face of adversity (2016, p. 91).

During Duckworth's talk, she encouraged the audience to calculate our grit scores based on a series of statements such as, "New ideas and projects sometimes distract me from previous ones" and "Setbacks don't discourage me. I don't give up easily." I found I was quite gritty. If you are a teacher, you probably are too. I became a full convert when Duckworth told us what grit was not. "Grit isn't talent," Duckworth said, "Grit isn't luck. Grit isn't how intensely, for the moment, you want something." For our students to become gritty and grow, we must applaud effort over talent and do our best to recognize our students' deepest passions as frequently as possible.

But, not everyone agrees. Noted educator and author Rick Wormeli has pushed back on the notion of grit as it is presented in many schools across America. He recognizes the good intentions at stake, but argues that an emphasis on grit should not foster disregard of racism, poverty, or social emotional issues. Wormeli explains, students who face obstacles "don't lack grit and tenacity," explaining, "They have plenty of it; that's how they survive. We lose all credibility by harping on it as the root of a student's problems. What these students lack are the resources, time, and support needed to maneuver, extend energy, and find hope in the instructional demands placed on them" (2021). Wormeli recognizes the limitations to affording second chances. The most important thing is to keep students from feeling like success is out of reach.

IN SHORT

- Do not praise natural ability or talent; instead, praise effort and students who seek out rigor.
- Remind students that it is possible to not be very good at something right now, but that does not prevent them from becoming skilled at that same task in the future.
- Self-control and perseverance are not enough if you wish to become outstanding at something; gritty individuals also possess passion.
- Before criticizing a student's lack of grit or inattention, consider their circumstances outside of school. They may be exceptionally gritty in their ability to simply survive.
- Give plenty of opportunities for second chances. Success should never feel entirely out of reach.

MODELS

The following models for growth will examine the ways in which we communicate with our students to help condition their mindsets. It won't take extra planning or grading to tweak your vocabulary, but it may get some getting used to. Remember to praise effort early and often.

Reward Growth

Devise a simple system to reward intellectual growth in your students. Allow opportunities for failure with feedback. Encourage risk-taking. Make time for practice. Most importantly, don't let grades suffer when students are making an effort, even if they aren't successful the first time. Try. Fail. Improve. Repeat.

I like to weigh assessments at the end of the semester more heavily than those in the beginning. Gradually increasing the weight of your assessments gives students an opportunity to adjust to your assessment style and master the course content. It also sends the message that it's acceptable to struggle or even fail at a task in the beginning if they are willing to work hard and make gains by the end of the semester. This way, a student who bombs the first assessment can recover by the time report cards drop.

It is increasingly common for elementary schools to use standards-based grading to reinforce the importance of growth and mastery. Rather than tabulating a content area grade out of 100% or employing letter grades, report cards are broken down into dozens of standards-based skills. In my experience, parents have a more difficult time making the adjustment to standards-based grading than students. Don't be surprised if a concerned parent calls to inquire how their perfect child could have possibly scored one out of four in "Matter and Energy in Organisms and Ecosystems." The teacher must explain that the science skill in question has not been covered in class yet, and therefore has not been mastered. This is no failure on the part of the child or the teacher—simply a matter of scope, sequence, and pacing. The benefit of standards-based grading is in the specificity of feedback. Rather than getting a *B* in Math, a parent can see that their child has yet to master "Number and Operations in Base Ten." In standards-based instructions, students are given multiple opportunities to demonstrate success until they master a skill.

I am also a huge proponent of the do-over. When students score below 80% on one of my assessments, I always allow them to come in for extra help and then try again to bring their grade up to 80%. If a student gets a perfect score on the do-over, I still only award them 80%, but the failing grade is obliterated. Not every student takes me up on my do-over policy. Even when students decline the opportunity to try again, I am reinforcing a growth mindset in my classroom by allowing do-overs. I am saying, "I value your learning more than I value your performance on one specific assignment."

One of my colleagues, Samantha Smith, reminded me that in her special education classroom, growth looks extremely different from student to student, and therefore rewarding growth also looks quite different from student to student. Some students are motivated by whole class incentives, while others just want a chance to listen to music once they've completed all of their work.

Smith has also encountered some special cases. "At the start of the year, I had a student who would tell me every single day that he would never learn math and he made sure the whole class heard him," said Smith. "I received no work from him and when I would sit with him, he would pretend he didn't hear me. I was beyond frustrated." Eventually, Smith pulled the student aside before class for a one-on-one conversation. "I told him it is my job to make sure he walks away with some skills. I told him that I was going to put him in a new seat to set him up for success. I told him it was not a punishment, it was my guarantee that he was in the best position for him to learn," she recalled (2021). The student sat in his new seat without objection, though he still refused to complete any work. "But, I noticed he had stopped ignoring me when I spoke to him," said Smith. "Then, about a week later, he called me over for help." At the end of class, Smith got everyone's attention and announced, "Hey, remember when he said he would never learn math? Well, I'm here to tell you that unfortunately that was not true; he has learned!" The class erupted into a large round of applause. Smith is proud to report the student has completed every assignment since then.

Gone are the days of striking fear into your students on the first week by administering an impossibly rigorous exam to set a serious tone. Growth mindset asks students to rise to the challenge. You will still encounter fixed mindset students who throw their hands up and surrender. "This class is impossible," they'll say. They may even declare that they are inept when it comes to your content area and they prefer not to try. Start with shorter assignments and quizzes, and then build up to longer ones as the year progresses.

Give Growth-Language Feedback

We've all done it—said things like, "Wow! You are one of the most talented writers I have ever had in the seventh grade," or "You are really smart at math!" I don't think we did any irreparable damage by swooning over our students, but we certainly didn't do them any favors. Praising natural talent prevents students from valuing effort. They may even avoid more challenging work because they fear failure and the realization that they weren't as smart as they thought they were. Better just not to try.

Focus on making small shifts in your language. Praise the process, not the person. Here are a few growth-mindset translations to get you started:

- "You must be really good at science." = "You must work really hard at science."
- "Math is so easy for you; you got a 100 percent on the math test." = "I can tell you studied hard for the math test."
- "You got it right. See, I knew you were smart." = "I liked watching you try a bunch of different approaches until you finally answered correctly."
- "This is going to be easy for you because you are so smart." = "This was a really difficult assignment, but you stuck with it and got it done."

- "You don't even have to try." = "That was too easy. Let's tackle something more difficult you can learn from."
- "You're not a math person." = "I appreciate your effort and I am going to stick with you until you understand this concept."

At the start of every lesson, I say my motto: "I believe in you. I think you can do it. I'm going to stick with you until you do." Like most things in my teacher tool belt, I borrowed the practice from an older and wiser teacher. Especially among middle schoolers, this daily affirmation can elicit some eye rolls at first, but I promise they come around eventually. Building a growth-mindset culture is a matter of normalizing failure and rewarding perseverance.

In Smith's special education classroom, the Structured Therapeutic Education Program, she faces very different circumstances from my own. "This grouping of students faces more emotional challenges," explained Smith. "Many of them struggle with confidence and working on a task for an extended period of time. They also struggle with being told that they did something incorrectly. For this reason, my class is structured very differently than most other classes." She prides herself on celebrating every little victory. I often hear Smith's voice spilling out of her room saying things like, "I love how you did (insert skill here), why don't you look at problems 3, 8, and 12 because they require that same skill. When you're done with those, let's talk about the skill that you will need for other problems" (2021). She is constantly setting students up for success.

When Smith needs students to fix a problem she might say something like, "You solved most of that problem correctly, but I did notice one mistake—I completely understand why you thought it was that way. Let's work together to fix it." She acknowledges there remains the occasional "meltdown" due to academic strains. "A meltdown is the perfect time for the student to work on coping skills with myself, the instructional aide, or the program behavior specialist," Smith reasoned. "During this time, we work on growth mindset or on coping strategies so they can learn how to appropriately advocate for what they need to be successful."

Promote Success Strategies

Growth language is not limited to written and verbal feedback. You can also incorporate growth language into your syllabus, your classroom decor, and your opening exercises. You have probably noticed the behaviors of your most successful students in previous years. Tell incoming students what worked for others in the past. Furthermore, tell them what helps you as a learner. Not every student will take your advice, but you will send a clear message that you value planning, strategizing, and working hard.

As a middle school teacher, I am accustomed to hosting a step-up day for incoming students from the local elementary schools. I always invite a few representatives from my class to be present on step-up day and field questions. Usually they provide helpful tips like, "Use an agenda to keep track of your assignments" and "Take advantage of opportunities to revise your work because it will help your grade go up." I find that incoming students are much more likely to learn from the success strategies of fellow students than they are from my own advice.

One activity I find particularly helpful at the start of the school year is asking students to outline an hour-by-hour schedule of a typical school day, including morning routines, after school activities, homework, and leisure time. Taking inventory of how students spend their time helps them make a direct correlation to their effort. If they set aside 30 minutes to study and then fail the exam, perhaps they need to increase the frequency or length of their study sessions in order to improve.

For students new to Smith's Structured Therapeutic Education Program, she seeks out models who are wonderful at showcasing their own successes in class. "You'd be surprised at how many students who understand a concept will reach out to struggling students and offer to help without being asked," said Smith. "I am honest about the fact that sometimes a student may be able to explain a problem better than I can and I give them the opportunity to try." As a special educator, Smith knows she cannot be everywhere at once. She encourages students waiting for support to seek help from more advanced learners who may be finished with their work.

"I like to think I've done a good job of modeling what helping looks like," she said. "I've always been a teacher who accepts quality over quantity and my students understand that early on." She makes sure to carve out a strong distinction between helping and copying. "They know that working towards learning the concept is worth more in my classroom," explained Smith. She relishes overhearing her students say things like, "You're almost right. Remember there are more negatives so our answer is negative." She admits that some students still struggle to model success for one another, saying things like, "Are you dumb? The answer is 10." This is when Smith takes the opportunity to step in and model a more appropriate response. "I will say things like, 'I think what (insert student's name) meant to say was, 'We should have multiplied, not added.' Why don't you take a second to multiply the problem and see if you got the same answer? Thank you for trying to solve the problem!'"

PRINCIPLES

You have probably had to find the strength to overcome challenges throughout your own academic career. Ask yourself:

When you faced failure in your own studies, what made you keep going? How did you persevere? Consider how you can pass those lessons along to your students while keeping the following principles in mind.

Design for Growth

Structure your course in a way that rewards effort and revision within reason. If you allow students opportunities to improve their grade on every assignment, you will never sleep again. Make small teaching adjustments to lighten the load. Designate a select number of assignments eligible for a do-over or revision. Weight your assignments more heavily at the end of a unit or grading period than you do at the beginning to allow students to calibrate their effort to meet your expectations. Use your first graded assignment as an opportunity to convey a growth mindset.

Communicate for Growth

Pay attention to the words coming out of your mouth in both formal and informal interactions with your students. Students should be able to tell that you value hard work and effort, just by looking at your syllabus. Hang anchor charts around the room with growth-mindset sentence frames to remind you and your students of what language to use.

Feedback for Growth

Summative assessments are inevitable. At some point you probably need to assign your student a grade. But, formative assessments are plentiful. Show confidence in a student's ability to succeed and be explicit about the level of effort necessary to do so. Leave comments alluding to the hard work that will be required on forthcoming assignments. Use growth language within all of your feedback.

SMALL TEACHING QUICK TIPS: GROWING

Use small modifications in your own language to strengthen the growth mindset among your students. Place value on effort and organization. Clearly articulate what it takes to be successful in your class and allow students to build toward your highest expectations.

· Ensure early success by intentionally sequencing your assignments to build to more challenging tasks. Reward students who take advantage of opportunities to revise. You don't need to award full credit for do-overs, just enough to reinforce their value.
· Use growth language when you give feedback to students. Show confidence in them and reiterate your belief that their hard work will pay off. Hang anchor charts throughout the room with examples of growth-language sentence starters and sentence frames.
· Share examples of your own failures that led to growth in your academic career. Ask top students to share their tips for your course with incoming students. Include your own success strategies right on your course syllabus.

CONCLUSION

Our mindsets shape the way we view exceptional individuals. I think this is particularly easy to see in our perceptions of pro-athletes or famous musicians. In one case, I collaborated with renowned artist Alice Mizrachi on an installation at our school and I made the mistake of saying in front of the whole class, "Alice, I wish I had your talent; I love art, but I'm not an artist." She just about lost her mind.

"When I was young, my parents were really strict with me," she explained. "They were so protective because they wanted to make sure their little baby girl was going to be kept safe. I spent most of my time at home and I would have to find things to occupy myself. As I began getting older, I realized that when I was in my room, instead of just sitting there I could create art. I discovered drawing and I thought, 'Wow, this is a really fun way to express myself.' I could create a whole universe in my own room. Almost like a fairytale universe that didn't allow me to feel so closed in. Drawing made me feel like I could travel to another dimension."

Mizrachi's passion for art gave way to perseverance. She spent every waking moment practicing her craft. "I knew that I enjoyed making art when I was five or six years old," she recalled. "But, I really got serious about it when I was in middle school. I had some great art teachers who encouraged me to paint and draw as much as I could. When I got to high school, my art teacher pushed me to apply to art school for university. That's where it really became clear that I was going to be an artist." Her teachers helped her to shift her mindset and believe in her own potential based on her willingness to work hard and strengthen her craft.

Mizrachi's parents discouraged her from enrolling in art school, but she applied anyway and was accepted to Parsons School of Design. She is a prime example of someone who was not born naturally talented; she worked for it. Today, you can find her murals in Amsterdam, Berlin, Tel Aviv, as well as dozens of major cities across America.

Chapter 10

Motivating

My students' motivations don't always match up with my own lesson plans. I find this to be particularly true in the one-to-one computing environment where students are more apt to fall down an internet rabbit hole and explore their deepest curiosities than confront whatever task I put in front of them. In most cases, I resist getting off-task and redirect them back to my assignment, but once in a while, these detours teach me a thing or two about what truly motivates the learners in front of me.

In 2015, I taught a third-grade technology course at a mid-sized suburban intermediate school in central Massachusetts. I had gotten comfortable as a middle school English teacher at the start of my career, and I was not accustomed to opening so many Capri Suns in the cafeteria or tying shoelaces on the playground. Nevertheless, an opportunity to work for my most respected mentor arose, and I agreed to give the younger grades a whirl. It was the school's first year going one-to-one with iPads, and I would be there to ease the growing pains for students and teachers alike. I had no idea what I was getting myself into.

Leading up to the new gig, I felt compelled by the research of Dr. Lisa Stoddard, a professor of environmental and sustainable studies at Worcester Polytechnic Institute. Stoddard's work recognized the perils of screen time. "We all love our screens: movies and sports on our flat screens, games, and Facebook on our phones, and Netflix on our iPads," she told me. "But, this shift in our work, school, and entertainment culture has led to kids ages eight to ten spending about eight hours per day on screens, instead of the two to three hours recommended by doctors; this shift in culture has also resulted in adults and kids spending less time outside in nature" (2018). Stoddard studied the direct links between a lack of access to nature and increasing rates of ADHD and childhood depression. She estimated that diagnoses of childhood depression doubled in the 2010s. "Research shows that when we expose and engage our kids in nature, there are multiple developmental, cognitive, emotional, and physical benefits," said Stoddard. "This includes improving their ability to concentrate, improved academic performance, reduced stress and aggression, improved social skills, and reduced risk of obesity, hypertension, and diabetes." As a new technology teacher, I was conflicted.

How could I reconcile the detriments of forced screen time during the school day with the benefits of state-of-the-art educational technology? After speaking with Stoddard at length, I got an idea. I proposed we would have technology class outside for as long as the New England climate allowed. Our access to mobile devices gave us great flexibility to morph into an outdoor course. I felt sure we could forge a deep connection with nature while leveraging a modern tool.

I began to familiarize myself with a very simple platform called MIT App Inventor with the idea of coding a basic application to help students learn about our environmental surroundings. They would collect natural artifacts, research the species they discovered on school grounds, and help me write basic code to launch an app. With a few exceptions, the kids were pretty jazzed to get outside and explore the local ecosystem.

Right away, I began to realize my own limitations. What did I know about classifying local plants? My students photographed over 25 different species of trees on day one, and I wasn't sure where to go from there. Meanwhile, building an app—no matter how simple—was more challenging than I had ever imagined.

Then, something strange happened. Just before the Thanksgiving break, one of my third graders arrived at school with a thick white binder full of old news clippings, maps, and photographs. "These belonged to my uncle," he told me.

I spent the whole vacation pouring over the binder. It turned out the 25 unique species of trees planted in rows outside my classroom window had not grown up by accident. Class after class, we had mulled about a bonafide arboretum planted by my student's uncle, James Courville. I had no idea.

"An arboretum is like a garden of trees," I explained to the third-grade students when we returned from break. We spread out a blanket under the bright yellow foliage of a ginkgo tree and I began to read aloud the story of James Courville.

"Courville taught science in our school building in the 1960s," I told them. "He was so bothered by the ugly dirt pit outside his classroom that he wrangled his students to fill in the hole, plant an expansive collection of trees, and assemble a corresponding field guide." I read aloud to them from one of the yellowed documents where he had written, "It will be a gift to our students and future generations." That last part sent a shiver up my spine. It was as if James Courville was speaking directly to me.

I looked at the semi-circle of cherubic faces. One of them yawned. Another one picked his nose.

"Isn't this exciting?" I asked them.

"Can we collect rocks?" the nose picker replied.

"Do you think we could get in touch with Mr. Courville?" I asked Courville's young nephew.

Before he could respond, a gregarious little redhead poked her head out from behind an iPad and said, "He's dead." The whole class gasped. "Drowned in a scuba accident," she told me, matter-of-factly.

Next, the effusive eight-year-old flipped her iPad around to display an obituary for one James Courville. Sure enough, the glowing screen revealed he had drowned in Provincetown on an oceanic expedition in 1978 when he was in his early forties. My stomach turned. Now, they were all listening.

"My dad says he buried an engine out here," Courville's nephew piped up. "His class had a funeral for it and everything."

I was even more confused.

"It's time to go inside," I told them. "Find your turn-and-talk partner to answer the discussion questions on our walk back." I hadn't bargained for a tragic scuba accident or a combustion burial ground; I needed to gather my thoughts and make a smooth transition. On the walk back through the arboretum, I could hear every single one of my students abuzz with excitement. It didn't stop there.

For the next week, I fielded questions to which I had very few answers. "It's a sad story, but it sounds like he died doing what he loved," I told them. "At least he passed away in nature." Their moony eyes stared up at me in horror.

Inspired by Courville's mystery, our app, which had been a boon to my students before these discoveries, became their greatest passion. We used a discussion protocol to come up with a concept and then set to work modifying a simple drawing application that students elected to name "Tree Trace." By the winter break, it was live on the Google Play Store. Players could trace the shapes of different leaves from the arboretum in order to identify each species. It was simple, yet engaging.

I thought Courville's family might be upset with me for dredging up old wounds, but instead, they thanked me for keeping his legacy and the arboretum alive. Come spring, my room was filled with students every lunch and recess period. They called themselves the "Maple Leaves" and even wrote a theme song about the arboretum. One of them brought in a metal detector so we could go out searching for the engine—a symbolic gesture Courville turned out to have orchestrated in condemnation of air pollution, long before his time. Another student convinced her father, a biology professor at College of the Holy Cross, to help us author an updated field guide. We even got an article about the arboretum published in the local newspaper. I scrambled to make sure all of these unplanned activities fit within the parameters of my technology curriculum. The kids continued to push for more.

In the end, we got in touch with many of Courville's former students and assembled enough donations to add our own tree to the arboretum. The emotional investment that Courville's story elicited was remarkable. Fear of my students' curiosities about his life and death had nearly caused me to veto the whole thing, but in the end, I was glad I let their motivations soar.

On the anniversary of his death that summer, I rode my bike out to the beach where his accident had taken place. I sat there for an hour, expecting to see a whale or some other miraculous display of nature. Nothing happened. I realized it was my curious students who had conjured Courville's magic. They had been determined to attempt academic feats far above their grade level and conquered one after another because of their steadfast motivation. No majestic whale sighting could ever top the wonder I had witnessed on their faces. I filled my pockets with rocks from the beach and when I got back to school, I placed one under each tree in the arboretum. Pride and grief welled up inside of me for a man I had never known.

The arboretum taught me not to diffuse the strong emotions of my students. Emotion is an effective pathway for practitioners of small teaching who are seeking to motivate their learners and themselves. You don't need to solve a half-century-old mystery to foster intrinsic motivation, but you shouldn't shy away from the opportunity if it presents itself. In this chapter, I explore how teachers can elicit and work with the emotions already present in their classrooms to give students frequent motivational bursts throughout the year.

WHAT'S THE THEORY?

Emotions like love and regret can interfere with our abilities as learners, or they can accelerate them. You've probably had an "aha" moment at some point in your life when emotions were running high. Maybe you decided to get out of a toxic relationship. Maybe you got an idea for the next great American novel. Or, maybe you decided you do like asparagus after all. Whatever it was, a strong emotion helped capture your attention. The same is true of our students.

Emotions can be aroused by sounds, pictures, sensations, and interactions. They can be conscious or unconscious. Regardless of where they come from, emotional reactions have a direct impact on our working memories. For this reason, teachers who learn to direct the emotions of their students can strengthen the neural pathways in a learner's brain to create long-term memories.

One recent study appearing in *Advances of Cognitive Psychology* examined the role of positive and negative emotions on working memory (Gokce et al., 2021). Researchers asked participants to play a memory game with task-irrelevant images designed to elicit negative, positive, or neutral emotions. The study revealed negative affective pictures reduced working memory capacity, while positive pictures increased working memory capacity compared to neutral images (Gokce et al., 2021). Furthermore, researchers concluded, "positive images elicit an approach reaction, where participants are more willing to deal with positive stimuli, while negative stimuli, in contrast, lead to an avoidance reaction" (Gokce et al., 2021).

I am not surprised by their findings. After all, I'm more likely to be on time for a class that makes me feel warm and fuzzy on the inside. I'm also more likely to sit up front, participate, and do my assignments when I feel a positive correlation with a particular teacher or subject. Emotions rule our motivations and therefore our capabilities to learn. Strong emotions result in sharp attention and heightened cognitive capacities.

Self-transcendence is one of the most powerful emotions in a learning environment. Highly motivated students often share a desire to help other people. A 2014 study titled "Boring but Important" looked closely at the types of purposefulness that inspire learners to persist (Yeager et al., 2014). Surprisingly, self-oriented motivations like individual career achievements or monetary success proved far less influential than self-transcendent motivations. Helping students recognize the ways in which their learning can change the world will make them more tenacious in their studies.

It's important to remember that establishing a self-transcendent purpose is a manner of organizing our goals, whereas reaching a specific goal or objective is a measurable achievement. In a conversation with director of the Purpose and Identity Processes Lab Anthony Burrow, podcast host Shankar Vedantam warned against conflating "goals" with one's "purpose" (2021b). Burrow and Vedantam agreed that doing so inevitably leads individuals to ask themselves "What will become of me once I've accomplished my goal?" Without a sense of purpose, successfully accomplishing the goal can actually leave our students feeling empty and directionless.

Olympian Michael Phelps famously struggled with this sensation throughout his career. "Really, after every Olympics I think I fell into a major state of depression," Phelps told CNN in 2018, adding that after the 2012 Olympics, he sat alone in his room for upwards of five days without food or sleep, "not wanting to be alive" (Scutti, 2018). Today, Phelps wields his power and influence to destigmatize mental illness and combat suicide. Winning a medal was his goal. Positively influencing America's youth is his purpose.

Burrow explains that while lack of purpose in young people looks like uncertainty, in adults it can feel like unending drudgery and routine. As teachers, it is just as important for us to find a sense of purpose in our work as it is for our students—sometimes even more so. "Purpose is a mood regulator in moments of stress or challenge," observed Burrow (Vedantam, 2021b). By finding self-transcendent purpose in our roles as educators, we are better suited to face adversity in the classroom.

Research shows that people with a stronger sense of purpose have greater interpersonal appeal, which leads to more opportunities and fulfillment. This is also true in our classrooms. To measure one's sense of purpose, Burrow suggests asking yourself, "Do you feel your life has a clear direction?" and "Do you feel your daily activities are engaging and important?" (Vedantam, 2021b). He reminds his listeners that cultivating a sense of purpose is a subjective experience that leads to a slower risk of cognitive decline. In the lower grades, a teacher could modify these questions to ask something like: "Do you have big plans for your life?" and "Do you feel like what you do every day is important?"

In other words, the cognitive benefits of finding your "why" is in your own control. Burrow describes the "why" as the orientation of a goal beyond oneself. This sense of purpose can be brought on in one of three ways: gradual self-discovery, a major life event, or drawing inspiration from someone else's example (Vedantam, 2021b). He concludes by saying, "Having a sense of purpose is associated with greater net-worth and lower levels of impulsivity" (Vedantam, 2021b). At the very least, we can model the cultivation of purpose for our students in the work that we do every day. At most, we can set students up for health and good fortune.

There is great value in expressing your own enthusiasm as a teacher. Your positive emotions carry over to your students. The more excited you are about teaching, the more social the learning experience becomes for your students. In her book, *The Spark of Learning: Energizing the College Classroom with the Science of Emotion*, Sarah Cavanagh describes a study in which, "The enthusiasm of the educators statistically predicted their students' ratings of enjoyment and perceived value in the subject matter" (2016, p. 64). Your own positive emotions toward learning are contagious. The same goes for your students. A few highly motivated students can energize an entire class, while a handful of yawning complainers can have the opposite effect.

I'm not suggesting you implement trust falls or daily renditions of "Kumbaya." The models that follow intend to provide an emotional boost and build a culture of lifelong learning in your classroom. Proceed at your own comfort level.

IN SHORT

- Emotional reactions have a direct impact on our students' working memories.
- Negative emotions have been found to reduce the working memory's capacity, while positive emotions increase its capacity.
- Strong emotions result in sharp attention and heightened cognitive capacities for the learners in our classrooms.
- Students who cultivate their larger purpose can use it to guide and organize their smaller goals.
- Ask students to reflect on the following questions to help establish a sense of purpose: "Do you have big plans for your life?" and "Do you feel like what you do every day is important?"
- Finding purpose beyond oneself slows cognitive decline.

- People with a sense of purpose have greater interpersonal appeal, leading to more opportunities.
- Purpose can be discovered through self-exploration, a major life event, or drawing inspiration from someone else.

MODELS

Emotions play a starring role in the adolescent experience. Even so, there are only a few career paths outside of teaching that rely on capturing those emotions rather than quelling them. Our society rewards silence and compliance. Let's be honest, most adults are fearful of provoking the untamed feelings of children. However, that is exactly how screenwriter Lisa Schultz Boyd spends her days in Hollywood. Boyd is one of the writers on *Star Trek: Prodigy*, a new animated television series on Nickelodeon. Like a teacher, Boyd's success hinges on her ability to communicate with young audiences in a way that plays to their emotions.

"It was most important to me and the *Star Trek: Prodigy* writing team to treat our young audience as smart enough to admire good art," said Boyd. "It helps that only a few of our characters were established previously—and we introduced our main crew of alien orphans for the first time" (2021).

Boyd set to work developing dynamic figures that Gen-Z could relate to. She grew particularly proud of the show's decision to include a non-binary character. "We made a point to give them their own choice of pronouns to use," Boyd said. "I believe young audiences will unconsciously recognize that and accept it as progress."

Boyd likes writing for children because she finds them especially astute. "I think it's often older audiences who are too set in their ways to appreciate originality and invention in the programs they're watching," said Boyd. "That's why, no offense to CBS procedurals, but older audiences are their most avid fans. *NCIS* scripts are structural, formulaic, easily packaged, and enjoyable content for what I call the average armchair detective." Boyd sees younger audiences as less frightened by risk-taking. "So long as their shows aren't too adult—violent or sexual," she specified, "they can understand drama, conflict, and suspense, and appreciate it in a way older audiences do not." Boyd loves to see kids rooting for complex characters and interpreting emotional consequences. "They have a fresh and biting sense of humor," she observed (2021).

Boyd relies heavily on her own tween-age daughter as a test audience subject for *Star Trek: Prodigy*. One especially helpful realization was that her daughter's favorite characters in books were often the villains with troubled backstories, not the prototypical heroes. "The villain in *Prodigy* is super awesome and cool and terrifying," she explained. "Without giving too much away, he is trying to right a wrong that happened in his past that caused the ruination of his home planet—he's not only scary, he's relatable" (2021).

Requiring students to memorize the capital of Ohio or self-explain an algebra problem won't help them if they don't care about a content area or if they believe they are incapable of learning from it. As teachers, we must strive to make our content relatable. Attitude is everything, including our own. We need to be inspired just as much as our students if we are going to survive in this profession. Like Boyd's confidence in her young audience's ability to recognize and appreciate complex art, we must trust in our students, stoke their curiosities, and fan the flames of inspiration. Small changes make a big difference.

You can activate emotions in your students such as curiosity and a sense of purpose, but you should also consider how to awaken emotions within yourself like enthusiasm and compassion. Motivate your class by charging the environment with beneficial emotions using the following models.

Positive Recognition

Relationship building won't add to your planning time or your grading load, but it will maximize any "free" moments of time you might have built into the school day. Instead of taking your frustrations home with you, spend spare moments during the school day positively acknowledging students in the halls. Try to learn as many names as possible, not just those of your students. Studies show that asking someone to introduce herself actually makes her more likely to speak up later. Special connections are built on recognition.

In addition to recognizing students, try to incorporate as much individual praise into your classes as possible. A recent Brigham Young University study found that praising middle school students improves on-task behavior by 60%–70%. "Students at high risk for emotional and behavioral disorders were also more likely to be on task, and their classroom marks went up by a full letter grade, compared to high-risk students in classrooms where teachers rarely offered praise" (Allen, 2021). BYU professor Paul Caldarella and his colleagues Ross Larsen and Leslie Williams completed the study in collaboration with Howard Wills at the University of Kansas. Similar findings were recorded among elementary students. "Even if teachers praised as much as they reprimanded, students' on-task behavior reached 60 percent," said Caldarella (Sorenson, 2020). Rather than calling out off-task students, praising on-task students sends the class into a productive frenzy.

Watch what happens when you start rattling off compliments while one student is misbehaving. "Great job, Amelia. Nice work, Asher. Excellent effort, Ezra. Well done, Slugger." Your mischievous students' jaws will drop.

"What about me, Miss?" they will ask you.

Keep the compliments rolling and watch how your trouble makers come to attention.

Literacy specialists Karin D. Wood and Janis Harmon go so far as to champion student recognition when it comes to the study of vocabulary. If we want students to possess the building blocks of language across all content areas, then we can't limit ourselves to memorizing vocabulary lists specified by Unicorn Math Company's aforementioned corporate materials.

"We believe a balance is needed in what teachers deem important and students feel is necessary, and there is ample evidence that giving students a voice in learning is intrinsically motivating, enhances learning, and increases the level of enjoyment and pleasure with the learning task," said Wood and Harmon (2020). The research shows that allowing students to preview a reading and pick out terms they deem significant will help them learn the words for life. Your positive recognition of their vocabulary choices is the first step toward helping them move new terms and definitions from their working memories to their long-term memory.

I once worked with a teacher who told students, "You have to date a word before you marry it." This comparison elicited snickers from middle schoolers, but the metaphor stuck. Wood and Harmon refer to this approach as aiming for "conceptually loaded" terms. "Effective vocabulary instruction must require students to apply the meanings of newly introduced terms in a variety of activities that build vocabulary literacy and consequently have a strong impact on comprehension" (Wood and Harmon, 2020). Sharing our decision-making process with students allows us to pierce through the surface-level understanding yielded from vocabulary recitation. Positive recognition of student decision making not only motivates our kids, it also maximizes learning outcomes.

It's never too early to start. "We provide immediate feedback for a job well done, a nice compliment given, following directions, etc." Central Massachusetts kindergarten teacher Jenny Bercume told me (2022). "We move a child's pin up on our pin chart. If a child's pin moves up twice in one day, I send home a purple heart with their positive behavior written on it." In Bercume's classroom, positive feedback far outweighs the negative. "We also use clothespins that have phrases on them such as 'I was a good friend' or 'I helped out!'" Bercume's students always enjoy showing off these simple accolades to their families.

Tell Great Stories

Take the advice of my editor and start with a story. Great stories invoke human emotions and therefore stick with us. You probably have plenty of stories up your sleeve based on the news, your travels, pop culture, and publications from great thinkers in your field. Be deliberate. Consider which of these stories will be strong enough to capture the attention of your students and then lead with it. Activate prior knowledge and emotions.

In my classroom, I used to begin every week with a grammar focus correction area. Students found these mini-lessons particularly dull. I am by no means a comedian, but I learned that kicking things off with a story helped students to stay engaged and retrieve the information later. Rather than boring them with a lecture about "your" versus "you're," I would tell them about a cow who misunderstood the farmer and met his tragic end when he was led into the barn and told, "You're dinner." Similarly, they get a real kick out of comma day when I reveal the age-old mix-up of "let's eat, grandma" and "let's eat grandma." Recycle your dad's old jokes.

Princeton Professor of Psychology Tania Lombrozo's work focuses on the human drive for explanation. She studies the ways in which storytelling helps us extract order and regularity from situations which might otherwise feel unsettling (Vedantam, 2021a). One of my middle school colleagues, Brian LaHair, relies heavily on storytelling in his creative writing elective. He insists that he is not the reason for his course's continued popularity, but rather the art of storytelling, which creates a hook to peak even the most reluctant students' interests. "Storytelling is akin to cooking," he explained. "A chef must first season the steak and preheat the grill before they begin cooking. The same can be said for education. Once the students are hooked, not only is a classroom community created, but students feel invested in the material. The learners begin to hang on every word as they wonder what will happen next in the curriculum" (2021).

LaHair uses storytelling to elevate student voice in the classroom by going out of his way to recognize each student as an equal shareholder in the learning process. "Students must feel safe to take chances and to ask questions," he said. "Without this, there are limited opportunities for student voice" (2021). LaHair is in the habit of creating inquiry at every turn by asking students to engage in regular exercises where they pose organic and unplanned questions. "By letting stream of consciousness questioning take place in my classroom, students are given the opportunity to engage with aspects of content that they might not otherwise come into contact with," said LaHair. That's when the human drive for explanation kicks in. Students use storytelling to extract order from the chaos of their questions, and LaHair watches their motivations soar.

Invoke Self-Transcendent Purpose

We all lose sight of the big picture from time to time. Assigning rigorous work is bound to elicit at least one pair of hands thrown into the air with a declaration that, "We're never going to need to know this." Chapter 7 emphasized the importance of establishing a broad year-long theme to unite all of your content and point to a larger purpose.

Beyond defining an overarching year-long theme and strong objectives on your syllabus, articulate how the subject matter will make a difference in the world. In the first edition of *Small Teaching*,

Jim Lang observed, "powerful pieces of writing or oratory have turned the tide against slavery, have created new nations, or have inspired people to drop everything and dedicate their lives to the poor" (2016). Frame your course as more than just a laundry list of content to consume. Present it as a blueprint to change the world around us.

Use the lofty life-changing goals from your syllabus to introduce daily lessons as well. Say things like, "Think of these presentations as if you are proposing a real solution to the City Council, because I'm planning to share the best ones with our local representatives." Building community partnerships is a great cheat code for creating a sense of relevance in your curriculum. I've even gone so far as to ask community partners to pen a strategic letter begging for my students' help. Without fail, the kids mobilize and pitch in just as they did to bring the arboretum back to its glory.

The trick to all of this is that it actually shifts the workload from you to your students and community partners. In my experience, they don't mind. It might take you 10 minutes to email the best slide presentation from your class to your local representative, but saying you were going to do so often means that a student poured additional hours into their work in hopes that someone from the real world would be affected by it. Likewise, community partners will take great lengths to please children and get a little press in return. You are the coach. Let them be the players and do the work.

Share Your Enthusiasm

Don't be afraid to show that you care. Nerd culture is everywhere right now. Tell your students you are "obsessed" with your subject matter. Lean into hyperbole. You've probably encountered at least one surly teacher who objected to putting on a show, but I bet that made their job pretty hard. I suggest you let your enthusiasm run wild. One of the perks of working with kids is that we're allowed to get silly.

Try to remember what it felt like to read your favorite book for the first time. Bottle that excitement because you are probably going to have to teach the same material until you can do it in your sleep. Resist going on auto-pilot. Teaching requires a fair amount of acting. It's not that we don't believe what we're saying; it's a simple matter of repetition. Think of each class as a performance, but remember you are not the main character.

Have you ever been to a hip-hop concert? Standard practice calls for a "hype person." The hype person encourages an audience to call and respond, cheer, and dance. Support your students by pumping them up. Model your genuine enthusiasm with the same dedication you would model your active reading skills. You are the hype person.

Show Compassion

We are all like icebergs. What we see on the surface cannot possibly convey the full weight of our emotions. Students will project their emotions in all sorts of ways, loud and soft. The next time a student takes a tone with you, try to remember how difficult it is to be young and show them the compassion they are searching for.

Today's curriculum leaves a lot more room for social-emotional learning than it did when *New York Times* best-selling author and illustrator Jarrett J. Krosoczka was coming of age. In his recent memoir *Hey, Kiddo*, he reflects on his experience growing up with an absent father and a mother struggling with addiction. Krosoczka had a hard time expressing his emotions as a boy, until his grandparents enrolled him in art classes.

"My grandparents, Joseph and Shirley, took me in just before my third birthday and raised me as their own," he told me. "They did so much to support and foster my creative efforts when I was growing up. They both lived to see me into adulthood, and they saw me publish several books" (Krosoczka, 2017). Krosoczka's success in the face of adversity is a direct result of the empathy and compassion of his grandparents and the art teachers of his youth.

Aside from sharing his story with young people through literature, Krosoczka has also delivered two very successful TEDx talks. "It's pretty crazy to think that over two million people have spent time listening to me deliver talks on the internet," he shared. "It's completely changed my life. On the surface, my TED Talks have elevated my profile, but more importantly, sharing my personal stories has connected me to people with similar experiences in ways that I never imagined possible" (2017). Krosoczka channels the compassion modeled for him as a young man and continues to touch the lives of countless youth.

Incorporating compassionate literature like *Hey, Kiddo* into our classrooms opens up opportunities to share our own stories and make our students feel supported. You never know what will stick with a kid for the rest of their life. Try your hardest to leverage the emotions present in your classroom in order to make a lasting positive impact.

PRINCIPLES

Allan Grigg, known to his fans as KoOoLkOjAk, co-wrote and co-produced a No. 1 Billboard hit single with Flo Rida. He worked on popular films including *The Hangover, The Lorax, 21 Jump Street*, and *Pitch Perfect*. He successfully collaborated with popular artists Nicki Minaj, Ke$ha, Waka Flocka Flame, and Britney Spears. And, throughout his entire career, he focused on just one thing: emotional impact.

Grigg understands the value of emotion in his art, but he never shies away from the fact that it's a job. "If you want to make an emotional impact, you need to bring forth your entrepreneurialism," he told me. "Study the greats. Study new artists, producers, and labels. Stay informed on the evolving climate of the biz"

(2017). Grigg recognizes the shared humanity in emotions, but also values his potential to motivate and influence others through their emotions. Teachers can do the same. The three principles outlined as follows will help inspire emotions in both you and your students. Strategically embrace the feelings that surface, rather than squashing them under your orthopedic teacher clogs.

Acknowledge the Emotions in the Room

You can't magic them away. Emotions run high when you put 20-odd children in a room together and tell them what to do. Take advantage of them. Heighten students' cognitive capacities by using jokes, songs, stories, and short videos throughout your lessons to capitalize on the motivation they inspire.

Make It Social

Emotions are even more contagious than yawns. Invite students into your direct instruction by allowing them to laugh, sigh, and cry freely. We are social animals. Encourage groups to work through negative emotions and ride the highs of success. If you find a class discussion taking a turn, see where it takes you. De-escalate as necessary, but remind students of how powerful emotions can be, both negative and positive.

Let Your Enthusiasm Show

If you don't care, neither will they. Children have an innate bologna meter. If you think your lesson is pointless, they will know. Show them your excitement. Try to channel the way it felt when you first discovered a love for your content area. Children are not empty vessels. Set a motivational tone to inspire learning by bringing energy and compassion to class every single day.

SMALL TEACHING QUICK TIPS: MOTIVATING

Not every kid is going to love your content area. They will, however, recognize your attitude toward that content area. Show enthusiasm for your work and student achievement will improve. Use these small, everyday motivational practices that have the power to boost engagement and learning.

- Learn everyone's name, including students you don't have in class. If you can't remember a name, make up a nickname. People love to feel recognized for a good reason. Acknowledge students who contribute and make it easy to do so. Praising students will keep them on-task more than scolding them will.
- Use storytelling to heighten the emotions of your students. They will be more engaged and more likely to remember your lesson.
- Explicitly state how the overarching goal of your course can help to change the world. Collaborate with community partners and make clear connections between learning and making a difference.
- Don't hide your enthusiasm. If students realize how much you care about your content area, they will be more likely to mirror your attitude and emotions.
- When negative emotions take hold of your students, show them compassion. It's hard to find motivation when you don't feel supported. Be the support person your most challenging student needs in their life.

CONCLUSION

There is a lot of fantastic research cited in the pages of this book, but it would be irresponsible to claim that we are nothing more than receptacles for neural networks. Emotions and attitudes intersect with both teaching and learning in our classrooms every day. Cultivating a sense of inspiration is just as important as fostering knowledge and understanding. We often describe students as being "emotional" or having an "attitude" with a negative connotation. This can be true. After all, every one of us has had to suck it up and go to school or work on a day when we weren't feeling well. On those occasions, we can agree, our effort suffers. I recently experienced this first-hand amid the challenges of virtual learning.

In December 2020, my husband got COVID. Everyone felt qualified to chime in about how the two of us should navigate our quarantine period under the same roof, but in the end, we took the advice of our City's Chief Medical Director and decided to isolate ourselves from one another. The week before the holiday break is always difficult as a teacher, but this was even worse than usual. My students were trapped behind a computer screen for virtual learning and I was separated from my husband by one big ugly wall.

"It's like I'm Kathy Bates in *Misery*," I called through the guest room door, every time I left him a cute little love note and a bowl of soup.

"Still not funny," he would respond.

I found myself distracted by his presence during the school day. Once, I thought I heard him crying out in pain, but it turned out he was just watching the "Fresh Prince of Bel-Air Reunion." To be honest, it was quite sad. RIP James Avery.

Every day, he would go for a walk in the yard. He thought it was cute to throw little rocks at my office window like Romeo while I was trying to administer exit tickets to my students or review my daily objective. "Sorry, I thought the class was over," he yelled up to the window. My students egged him on. I'm pretty sure he was just hungry for attention.

I started to worry about his dishes, but he told me they were all "taken care of." I suspected they were piling up in a bin in the closet, so I left a sponge and some dish soap outside his door during my lunch break. He told me they smelled "fine," but

I read that loss of smell was a COVID symptom. Come to think of it, he also claimed he no longer required deodorant. Something about resetting his skin's "natural microbiome?" I cried foul.

I continued to test negative, but my professional focus was lost. During a Zoom faculty meeting, I ordered a Wilson volleyball off Amazon. When it arrived the next day, I painted a face on it so he would have a friend like Tom Hanks in the movie *Cast Away*.

At first, I didn't want to share what was going on at home with my students. When I finally fessed up and told them about my "patient" in the next room, they were very empathetic.

"I thought something was off," one of them told me, matter-of-factly.

They always know.

The students in your class are probably facing a whole host of distracting obstacles. Maybe they struck out on the ball field or at the school dance. Maybe they are in a fight with their best friend. Maybe a major world event has got them doubting the future of humanity. Whatever it is, it's best if they can acknowledge their attitudes and emotions.

In researching peer-to-peer connections, I corresponded with Laurie R. Santos, the professor of Yale University's most popular course in history, which focuses on the science of happiness—my favorite emotional state. "There's evidence that a positive mood can boost creativity, so I think it's definitely something to incorporate more often into the classroom experience," Santos told me. She places particular emphasis on the importance of gratitude in her own class as a means for increasing her students' learning capacity.

> First, I have students perform what's called a gratitude list. For seven days, students are asked to write down at least five things for which they are grateful. They can be little things or big things. Students are also asked to do what's called a gratitude visit. Students are told, "Think of

one person, still living, who made a big difference in your life but whom you never properly thanked. Find a quiet spot when you have a half-hour and write a 300-word, heartfelt testimony to that person, explaining how he or she touched your life and why he or she is meaningful to you. If you'd like to take it to the next level, schedule a time to visit this person by phone or Zoom and share your letter." Gratitude is a powerful tool for increasing happiness because it intensifies positive memories and forges social bonds. (Santos, 2021)

We have to be purposeful when it comes to manipulating student emotions in the classroom. Bringing everyone to tears or hysterics every day won't do you any favors. Emotions can accelerate learning just as easily as they can offset it. Positive emotions like gratitude, amazement, and astonishment have the ability to motivate our learning. Even negative emotions like bewilderment or embarrassment can sometimes drive us to work harder and overcome our weaknesses. Feeling something is half the battle. The students who will have the most trouble finding inspiration are those who suffer from apathy and indifference.

Chapter 11

Expanding

After 12 years of teaching, it finally happened; I got called to the vice principal's office. She held up a pink pamphlet with a hand scrawled title that read, "How to Respect Girls and Women (Plus People in General): A Basic Guide." One of my students made it for extra credit in response to the novel we were reading, which touched on some basic tenets of feminism. I made copies.

"Do you recognize this?" the vice principal asked me.

"Yes," I said.

"Did you make copies of this for a student?"

"Yes, I did," I told her.

"Do you realize that means you were distributing propaganda on school grounds?" she asked.

"Feminist propaganda?" I replied, half joking.

"Yes," she said firmly.

The pamphlet contained helpful tidbits such as, "Treat women like human beings" and "You need to listen to what women say about their bodies and respect their natural functions." My favorite section boldly stated, "The way a woman dresses does not give consent for one to touch them and make them feel uncomfortable, ever." The word *ever* was capitalized and underlined twice.

"I don't mean to be disrespectful, but I guess I'm just proud of them," I told my vice principal.

She sighed. "You're not in trouble," she said, "just destroy the rest of the pamphlets. Get rid of them. Make this go away."

I was mortified. This was not a problem small teaching could fix. It was too infuriating, too complicated, too messy. Worst of all, the well-intentioned author of the pamphlet had gotten wind that I was feeling the repercussions of her bravery. As proud as she had made me hours before when she handed me the pamphlet—now, she was feeling small and vulnerable. We needed a big teaching fix.

Teaching innovation often begins with small adjustments, but I should warn you—small changes have a funny way of expanding. After pamphlet-gate, my students became fixated with raising their voices for the entire community to hear. To avoid overextending myself, I called in the reinforcements. As I mentioned in Chapter 8, there are a lot of community partners who want to help school children, or at least get some good press. Large districts have grant offices to point you in the direction of funding. When all else fails, I ask the kids to write up a little something for DonorsChoose and hope some billionaire in need of a tax write-off will bite.

Through the grant office in my district, I was connected with our local Cultural Council who suggested we work with Harbor Voices. Harbor Voices is a Massachusetts based nonprofit that specializes in turning stories into art. "One of the most important things to the work is the people who are involved—people who are interviewing others or are interviewing each other or are the interviewees—all manage to connect to one another through shared experiences," explained Executive Director Stephanie Benenson (2021). "Through this artistic and creative process, students are discovering that there are others who are facing similar obstacles and they have found a networking community of support."

I knew right away that if anyone could help my students amplify their voices, it would be Benenson. She helped me teach students to conduct interviews based on the theme of their choosing: "Not Alone."

Students captured reflections on anxiety, body image issues, relationships, depression, and the general angst of being a middle schooler. Benenson edited together a sound cloud and synced it with a laser show for us to present to the school community.

The night of our art installation was electric. One family brought dumplings and egg rolls for the whole class. Dozens of local artists came out to show their support. We all wore matching tie-dyed T-shirts with quotes from the installation written on the back. My students felt like their voices finally mattered, and they were right. Our "Not Alone" installation was the result of big teaching. I stayed at school late every day. I wrote additional grants to help cover our costs. My hands were purple for a week from the tie-dye. But, it was totally worth it because I wanted to go big. I found my motivation. I felt a strong sense of purpose.

I am in the practice of asking students to reflect after milestones big and small. Following the "Not Alone" installation, my class wrote a poem together to reflect on our capital B-I-G project. I have never been more proud and inspired as an educator.

Not Alone
Grade 7 Class of 2021

Students arrive and we're feeling alright,
Unsure of what to expect in the light.
But, the art persuades us even before
Sharp colors swirl to reveal what's in store.
Thoughts run through our heads,

And feet run through the field.
Our love makes it clear,
We've all come to heal.
We open our ears,
Color beams dance,
Clouds move in fear,
This is our chance.
Lasers drift across the sky,
Our words striking the air.
Together, we take in the show
And remember what we share.
Our voices begin speaking,
And there's quiet from the crowd.
We touch them with our confidence,
They hear us, clear and loud.
Contrast in the dark night,
Like a firework finale.
Flashes, wordful as they move,
We shine hope around The Valley.

MODELS, PRINCIPLES, AND RESOURCES

Since the big teaching models that are suggested in this chapter represent unique approaches to pedagogy, they each appear with their corresponding theory and principle rather than in a separate section. In addition to the theories, models, and principles to help you expand your practice, I am including suggested resources to help you expand your thinking about teaching big and small.

Project-Based Learning

Project-based learning asks students to collaborate and address a challenge over a sustained period of time, then present a solution to the public. This can take place at virtually any grade level. First graders can collect data and develop a plan to reduce their classmates' impact on the environment. Fifth graders can assemble a financial plan to start saving for their futures. Eighth graders can revamp the grading system to better reflect the modern workplace. The possibilities are endless.

A great resource for working backward to expand upon your learning objective is the Harvard University database ABLConnect. Teachers can browse by activity, subject, time frame, or my favorite—learning goal. The site is a hotbed of project-based learning, as in real-world applications of in-class concepts and skills.

My students' decision to tackle the silencing of youth voices by creating an art installation is an example of project-based learning. We were able to master the Common Core ELA Standards and form connections to our assigned reading, while addressing a real-world problem. Students prepared for and participated in a range of conversations and collaborations with diverse partners, building on others' ideas and expressing their own ideas clearly and persuasively. Furthermore, they made strategic use of digital media and visual displays to express information and enhance understanding of their presentations. The energy and interest I witnessed during this project made the demands of project-based learning more manageable for me.

The goal of project-based learning is to extend student work beyond the classroom and into a public space. We moved beyond the school community in order to impact the larger neighborhood and its inhabitants. If you can design a project, or even better, have students design a project that requires a public showcase, they are bound to build connections between your discipline and the world around them. Beyond invoking purpose, project-based learning demands motivation and creativity. Project-based learning also requires many small teaching practices and culminates in a big teaching result.

Principle Students will need to look outside of your course for project-based learning inspiration. Student ownership is key to making project-based learning manageable. Fair warning: Every time I have been too heavy-handed in guiding a final project, I end up doing the bulk of the work. Instead, allow a democratic process to take place. Use a Google Form to survey the class. Or, post student's project ideas on chart paper throughout the room and give students two stickers apiece to cast their votes. I tell students they cannot vote for their own idea, but they are allowed to put both stickers on one piece of chart paper to show double the support. In the end, the visual impact of a piece of chart paper covered in the most stickers will help students to identify their shared interests and build momentum. Visit Harvard's free ABLConnect database for excellent inspiration and examples.

Community Service Learning

Community service learning (CSL) takes project-based learning a step further. The KIDS Model begins with a game that asks students to differentiate between community-based learning, community service, and community service learning (Harkins Consulting, 2021). Community service is an activity designed to address the needs of a school or community, while community-based learning is an approach that relies on local organizations and individuals to enhance the curriculum. The KIDS (Kids Involved Doing Service-Learning) model defines *CSL* as, "A method of teaching and learning that challenges students to identify, research, propose, and implement solutions to real needs in their school or community as part of their curriculum" (Harkins Consulting, 2021). In order to constitute CSL, the project must offer academic integrity, student ownership, and apprentice citizenship. In order to help you distinguish between CSL and its counterparts, I have provided an example of each below:

· A community service project at an elementary school asks students to organize a coat drive during the winter months for a local shelter.
· A community-based project invites a member of the chronic homelessness task force into an elementary school class to discuss the struggles faced by homeless individuals in a community.
· A CSL project asks students to read a story about a man without a home, "The Treasure of Lemon Brown," by Walter Dean Meyers. Next, students research houselessness in their own community and propose a variety of solutions to the problems faced by individuals without homes. Finally, students partner with the chronic homelessness force to educate the community about homelessness.

All three of these terms are commonly confused. Helping students to first understand what sets apart CSL will strengthen your future CSL project.

In Chapter 8, we discussed the importance of establishing a self-transcendent purpose to drive the learning that takes place in our classrooms; CSL inspires self-transcendent purpose among students in a structured way. Remember, CSL requires academic integrity, student ownership, and apprentice citizenship.

Learners should discover and investigate a problem or need, research and design solutions, plan and implement a project, and evaluate their impact. All the while, students should be reflecting, collaborating, celebrating, and publicizing their work. As the teacher, your greatest responsibility is to build explicit connections between your curriculum standards and the student-driven project.

The National Youth Leadership Council has done a nice job designing standards for quality practice. The NYLC standard for Link to Curriculum states, "Service-learning is intentionally used as an instructional strategy to meet learning goals and/or content standards." In some cases, students will identify a problem themselves based on a variety of options embedded within your course content. In other cases, your course content will present a specific problem and they will identify a variety of possible solutions. In both instances, your most important role is to access the curriculum standards while providing students with a voice to feel empowered.

Principle Community service learning is intimidating. There's a reason student agency and community partnership are pivotal to CSL; they allow you to divvy up the work. When students make decisions about the direction the project is going, they will be more likely to shoulder the workload. Likewise, hooking the right community partner will lead to valuable resources and logistical management. Your job should be to worry about maintaining academic integrity. Let your students and community partners take care of the rest.

I also recommend seeking out someone in your building who has pioneered CSL in their own classroom. Surprise them with their favorite candy bar or latte and then coerce them into telling you all of their CSL secrets. Don't limit them to their successes; ask about their failures as well and what they wish they knew when they were starting out.

My most fruitful tactic when it comes to attracting community partners is to have students reach out with a handwritten letter. Even the shrewdest executive will have a tough time saying no to the query of an adorable youth on a mission. Make a short list of prospective community partners to help you achieve your goal, and then give students an opportunity to pitch the project in their own words. Organizations and businesses will be much more likely to respond to a child than an adult.

Games and Simulations

Anything can be gamified. I once watched a fifth-grade teacher convince her entire class to feverishly clean up her classroom while playing a game she called "Magic Trash." Every student was charged with picking up ten pieces of trash off the carpet in hopes they would select the "magic" piece of trash that the teacher had predetermined. Whomever had the "magic" trash at the end of clean up time received a prize. They would beg to play every Friday. When she left for the weekend, her room was always spotless.

Role-playing historic events or recreating scenes from a novel can also be effective forms of play. In her book *When Kids Can't Read, What Teachers Can Do*, Kylene Beers suggests students create tableaus of important moments in the books they are reading by dressing up, designing props, and choreographing action on multiple planes (2003). I like to let students apply Instagram filters to the photos they capture of their tableaus and write a corresponding social media caption. This added step not only increases engagement, but also helps them delve more deeply into characterization. I've overheard numerous conversations go something like:

> "What would Edgar Allen Poe's aesthetic be?"
> "I think he'd go with Dark Academia."
> "No way. He'd definitely be more of a Lofi guy—real grainy and black and white."

A few years ago, I invited video game designer Ryan Canuel into my fourth-grade technology class as a guest speaker. Canuel is the co-founder and CEO of Petricore, Inc., an interactive software development company based out of Massachusetts. Petricore has worked with more than 40 museums to create simulations reflective of people's stories. "We made a game where you played as a Native

American through three periods in history to help players better understand the Native American experience," he told the class (2018).

Petricore's process is reminiscent of project-based learning. "The way that we come up with our games is that we do a game jam," said Canuel. "We come into the office, lock ourselves in a room and throw out as many interesting ideas as we can. We pitch around different games and then build a prototype—a very basic version of the game that won't look anything like our finished product, but it allows us to test things out and see what will work and what won't" (2018). Like Magic Trash, Canuel excels at turning unwelcome obstacles into entertaining games. His popular game Battery Boy actually changes based on the battery life of the device you are playing on. "As your battery starts to die, the game will get harder," he explained (2018).

While Canuel's career quite literally centers on games, the features of almost all "work" are strikingly similar to the common features of games. The defining features of games and work are very similar, but one is pleasurable and one can often feel undesirable. Wharton School Professor Ethan Mollick points out the paradox that many dimensions of games look a lot like work (Vedantam, 2021c). The primary difference between a game and work is liability. The cost. Failing at a game has little or no impact on our lives, while failing at a career has life-altering consequences.

Games use storytelling and systems of failure that allow us to learn from mistakes and try again. "Games lend themselves very naturally to thinking about systems and how they break and how they fail," explains Mollick. "And then, you get the real sense of improvement from that failure in games that you don't in real life. If your startup company fails, that feels pretty bad. But if it fails in a game, maybe that was interesting" (Vedantam, 2021c). Similarly, the high stakes of a summative assignment can make students much less willing to take risks or discuss their failures, whereas in games, failure is compelling.

Mollick points out that humans love the illusion of danger or pain without actual danger or pain. That's why people willingly jump out of airplanes every day. Games and simulations have the same effect. "I mean in the most basic sense, learning is about failure and about doing things better the next time," said Mollick. "It's why testing helps us learn better. In the most basic sense, learning is about failing and trying again" (Vedantam, 2021c). Framed as games and simulations, classroom assessments can have the same engaging effect.

Games are designed for flow. Levels get harder and harder until you lose. Entering a state of flow, in which a task is difficult enough for you to stay engaged and not so hard that you become overly frustrated, is very difficult to achieve in real life. "The sense of accomplishment is something that you can get in a game where everything is always calibrated to keep you in that flow state," explains Mollick (Vedantam, 2021c). I don't care if you love your job, the teacher's room has free snacks, and your principal walks on water—there's no workplace in the world where employees maintain a state of flow 100% of the time.

Work cannot adjust its difficulty level to keep us engaged without getting stressed or bored, but schoolwork can. Mollick hopes to use games to identify entrepreneurial talent among his students at the Wharton School. He notes that while many parents and educators worry about the violent and addictive nature of games, there are companies using the psychology of games to improve job readiness and education. One example is Foldit, a game used for citizen science to outsource complex tasks to regular people. "The most successful teams at folding proteins are actually the teams that don't have any formal biology training," observed Mollick. "So, it's really interesting because these teams would never have been drawn to the problem if it hadn't been turned into a game" (Vedantam, 2021c). The gamification of tasks, like in Foldit where online players fold proteins, takes elements of games and applies them to aspects of work.

Many companies, like Microsoft, use gamification internally to employ tactics such as badging and credentialing. Mollick reports that as a result, programs are being released more quickly and with fewer bugs at Microsoft (Vedantam, 2021c). In badging and credentialing systems, workers are acknowledged and rewarded publicly with a graphic representation of their achievements. You've probably seen badges in a colleague's email signature from entities such as Google for Education.

The practice of using games in the workplace is not brand new. In fact, the Top Gun simulator was one of America's first big success stories. During the Vietnam War, the Air Force and Navy both noted that pilots were underperforming. The Air Force used its resources to upgrade equipment, while the Navy launched Top Gun in order to expose novice pilots to dire conditions. According to Mollick, practicing with Top Gun proved far more effective than splurging on new planes (Vedantam, 2021c). Simulations and games have since become critical job training elements in fields ranging from medical training to truck driving. It's simple. Players who practice enough simulations find their skills are transferable to the real world.

If your students are bringing history or politics to life in a simulation, the outcome of their role-play does not necessarily have to be an accurate reflection of reality. I am especially fond of the chaos that ensues throughout the Apple TV documentary *Boys State*, which chronicles a group of teenage boys in Texas put through a simulation to design a representative government from scratch (Moss and McBaine, 2020). In the end, only one can be Governor and the competition is stiff. The simulation is by no means a parallel to the historic elections of Texas. Instead, the boys embark on a fresh path to explore their possibilities. If you're curious whether it worked, take a moment to peruse the alumni list of *Boys State* programs from across the country. Notable high-school–aged participants who attended in the past included: Neil Armstrong, Jon Bon Jovi, Cory Booker, Michael Jordan, and Bruce Springsteen. If allowing simulations to play out in our classrooms could produce the next MJ or The Boss, what are we waiting for?

Principle During games and simulations, your role is that of coordinator or coach. Students will play their parts and follow the rules you define for them. Provide clear parameters and let the constraints of the game ignite their creativity. With that, be mindful of what you are asking students to embody. I was absolutely horrified during my first year of teaching when a social studies instructor in the next room conducted a slave auction in his class. When I told him as much, he didn't speak to me for months. I still think regularly about the negative repercussions his simulation exercise had on students. Consider the potential for trauma triggers before you request students to play along.

Barnard College's Reacting to the Past Consortium is a highly respected resource for role-playing games. It may already offer a game in your content area that suits your curriculum, although it tends to be fairly expensive if you are covering the cost yourself. Virtual labs are plentiful online, and many science textbooks include simulations along with their ebooks. The game you are looking for probably already exists, so don't feel compelled to recreate the wheel.

When I make my own virtual games for class, I like to use Gimkit or Kahoot!. Gimkit mimics a variety of popular video games like "Among Us," but allows questions to be modified and customized to your own content. Kahoot! is more akin to a game show, though it is certainly an improvement on the PowerPoint Jeopardy activities of yesteryear.

Resources

I try to read at least one new book on education every year, but if I'm being honest, a lot of my independent professional development takes place on my phone. Social media allows me to curate my own personal learning network made up of my favorite teaching experts. I also subscribe to email newsletters, which keep my inbox full of the most poignant research and ideas in education.

Books Dozens of great books on education are published every year. You can download many of them straight to your phone with the Kindle app, or listen during your morning commute with Audible.

· *Teach Like a Champion 3.0* (Doug Lemov, 2021). Lemov outlines specific techniques employed by high-performing teachers. In the newest edition, he pays particular attention to diversity, equity, and inclusion in education.
· *Notice & Note: Strategies for Close Reading* (Kylene Beers and Robert E. Probst, 2012). A step-by-step guide to cultivating critical reading habits and close reading strategies among reluctant readers.
· *Grit: The Power of Passion and Perseverance* (Angela Duckworth, 2016). The secret to achievement surpasses natural talent. Excellent learners, athletes, and educators combine passion and long-term persistence to reach the highest echelons of success.
· *Fair Isn't Always Equal* (Rick Wormeli, 2006). An analysis of assessment practices in the differentiated classroom, including redos, scaling, and effort-based grading.
· *The Creativity Code: How AI is learning to write, paint and think* (Marcus du Sautoy, 2019). Why should we be emphasizing

creativity in classrooms? Du Sautoy explores the implications of artificial intelligence on the future of teaching.

· *Uncommon Sense Teaching: Practical Insights to Brain Science to Help Students Learn* (Barbara Oakley, Beth Rogowsky, and Terrence Sejnowski, 2021). A scientific deep dive into the brain brimming with easy-to-understand metaphors. My biggest takeaway is that the best teachers know how to transfer knowledge from working memory to long-term memory.

Web Resources Particularly during the school year, I rely on a variety of online resources to help me stay current in my field. I like to spend the first 20 minutes of my morning, before students arrive, checking in with my favorite outlets. I also find myself scrolling through them on my phone while I'm waiting in line at the grocery store.

· *ABLConnect*: https://ablconnect.harvard.edu/ A Harvard University website, frequently updated to provide concrete strategies for activity-based learning.
· *Learning for Justice:* https://www.learningforjustice.org/ Free educator resources to supplement your existing curriculum, designed to advance human rights.
· *Facing History and Ourselves*: https://www.facinghistory.org/ Resources designed to examine how past decisions and pivotal moments in history will lead to the decisions students will confront in their own lives.
· *Google for Education* teaching resources: https://edu.google.com/ Lesson plans designed by Google to inspire creativity, encourage hands-on learning, and equip students with digital skills.
· The *Marshall Memo:* https://marshallmemo.com/ This newsletter provides a round-up of important ideas and research in K–12 education, curated by Kim Marshall from the 150 publications he reads every week.

Social Media Social media allows educators to peek inside the classrooms of veteran teachers around the world for inspiration and professional development alike. Begin building your network with a few of my favorite experts:

· Dr. Catlin Tucker on Twitter: @Catlin_Tucker Blended learning coach and best-selling author Catlin R. Tucker shares practical resources for the contemporary classroom.
· Yesenia Villar on Instagram: @yesenia.villar. An account dedicated to uplifting Black, Indigenous, and People of Color (BIPOC) in Library and Information Sciences. Villar is an anti-racist librarian who builds community and creates space for BIPOC educators to mentor, collaborate, and innovate.
· Heidi on TikTok: @learningwithheidi This Wisconsin-based first-grade teacher shares the science of reading in short engaging videos, including quick tips for reading instruction and building phonemic awareness.
· Education Week on Twitter: @educationweek An empowering account that aims to inspire K–12 teachers with news, analysis, and opinion.
· Apple Education: @AppleEDU Apple's education-focused Twitter feed sparks news ideas and "aha!" moments for innovative teachers.
· Nicholas Ferroni on Twitter and Instagram: @NicholasFerroni Okay, okay—Yes, Ferroni was named "Sexiest Teacher Alive'" by *People Magazine*, but that's not the only reason I follow him. Ferroni is also an outspoken advocate for LGBTQIA+ youth and founder of "Teach the Truth," a campaign to incorporate more women and people of color in social studies curriculums.
· Finally, I invite you to join the ongoing discourse about #small-teaching by following me on Instagram (@sarah_connell), Twitter (@sconnell410), and TikTok (@sarahconnellsanders).

SMALL TEACHING QUICK TIPS: EXPANDING

There is too much information out there to consume everything. Hold yourself to a realistic expectation and commit to a manageable professional development goal. If you made it this far, odds are you probably enjoy aspects of teaching and want to continue improving your craft. Don't be a stranger.

- Set a goal of reading at least one new book on education per year.
- Attend a teaching conference. If your district won't pay for it, then offer to present or facilitate a session on something you could do in your sleep. Presenters are typically given free entry to all of the conference offerings.
- Subscribe to a newsletter like the *Marshall Memo* for a curated selection of relevant articles.
- Create a personal learning network on social media by following specific hashtags such as #smallteaching, #edchat, #teaching, and #learning.

CONCLUSION

A 2021 survey conducted by the RAND research organization found that compared to the one in six teachers likely to leave the profession annually prior to the pandemic, one in four are now likely to walk away from teaching each year (Steiner and Woo, 2021). Another survey of nearly 10,000 teachers conducted by the American Psychological Association between July 2020 and June 2021 found that almost half of all teachers reported they desire or plan to quit or transfer their jobs due to concerns about school climate and school safety.

We are exhausted. Working conditions are more stressful than ever. On top of that, the survey found that a much higher proportion of teachers reported symptoms of depression than the general adult population. Just as my students reminded me at the end of the last school year, "You are not alone."

If the prospect of overhauling your entire course scares you, know that you're not alone. Start by making small changes. Even big teachers require the building blocks of small teaching to achieve their goals. In fact, big teaching can't exist without the fundamentals. I've always appreciated the sage advice of human rights activist Desmond Tutu, which says, "There is only one way to eat an elephant: a bite at a time." Think of big teaching as your proverbial elephant. Don't rush the process. Take it bite by bite. . . .

The goal of this book is to persuade you to keep going. You can command incredible learning outcomes through small, every-day decisions you make in your course design, communication style, classroom practices, and the way you approach roadblocks. Small adjustments can make a huge difference. Don't be afraid to abandon any strategies I have presented that don't work for you. Adjust them to your own style and needs.

Sometimes, the best small teaching practices are taking place in the classroom right next door. If you have to attend weekly meetings for a Professional Learning Community or mandated Professional Development, arrive with an open mind. You don't need to make big changes. Listen for the small tips and tricks that are actively making your colleagues' lives easier, and then see if they can work for you.

You probably have a class tomorrow morning. Begin with the first six minutes. Ask students to practice retrieval by recalling information from a previous lesson. Or, have them make a prediction based on their prior knowledge of a new topic. Try to engage with a handful of students individually and get to know what they are passionate about.

Maybe you're not ready to start tomorrow, and that's okay too. Start thinking about your syllabus for next semester or next year.

What year-long theme will tie your course together with purpose? What advice do the most successful students in front of you right now have for the students who will be in your future classes? How can the language on your syllabus better reflect a growth mindset?

Finally, if you decide to continue your teaching career, whether it be for one more year or 30 more years, institute your own growth mindset. Don't downplay your victories, even if you start by making just one small change. Push yourself to continue learning and your job will get easier. You have reached the end, and so, I ask you: Where will you begin?

Chapter 12

Putting It All Together: Matt Halpern, Kindergarten Teacher and Literacy Consultant

M att Halpern brings nearly two decades of experience in K–2 education to the table. A few years ago, he began presenting and consulting during his summer breaks. Amid the challenges of the pandemic, he left his classroom in coastal Maine to consult full time on behalf of his private business Matt Halpern Education. Today, Halpern works with school districts across the country and industry leaders like Scholastic. His first book, *A Teacher's Guide to Interactive Writing*, is forthcoming from Heinemann. I was particularly eager to speak with Halpern because much of my background is in the intermediate and middle grades. He helped me envision what many of our small teaching principles look like for younger students.

How do you post a daily agenda for students who haven't yet learned to read?

For kindergarten and first grade, a schedule or an agenda for our day has pictures. It will have writing as well, but it's definitely going to have a picture. Usually what I would do is use an original photograph. If it says "read aloud," there's going to be a picture of me doing a read aloud. If it says "phonics," there's going to be a picture of an activity that kids would associate with phonics. When it's time for us to do math, it's going to be a picture of a math activity. I provide something kids can recognize without necessarily being able to read. We also read through our schedule together each day. Ultimately, they learn to read what it says. But, that takes time. Right? Instead of me just posting an agenda, I prefer to write it as I'm saying it. It helps kids make meaning. And I might even ask them what picture we could use for different activities. Like, "Independent reading. What would that look like?" I'm not an artist at all, but I can manage a quick drawing of one person with one book to show independent reading, and then I write it out as well.

Is that also how you share your learning objectives?

Yes. Consistency is the most important thing. I have used the Lucy Calkins and Teachers College Units of Study, which I know people have all kinds of thoughts about. I'm not here to say whether they're great or not. But, one of the things that they do well is to use routine language. You start every lesson by saying, "Today, I want to teach you . . ." We would use the same language every day.

What does project-based learning look like for little kids?

I worked at a project-based learning school early in my career. And when I started at the school, I knew nothing about project-based learning. They sent us to project-based learning training from Buck Institute. The whole time I was kind of asking the same question as you, "How the heck are my kindergarteners going to do this?" At the beginning of the year, I found it was a lot more teacher directed. We didn't know each other yet, but I was still trying to give them voice and choice in the process. At the beginning of the year, I would ask something like, "Do you think we could learn about the life cycle of a butterfly so much that we could teach it to our families?" By the middle of the year to the end of the year, I would have the kids picking projects of their own. For example, our school was in the middle of a neighborhood. A lot of people from the community used the playground even if they didn't go to the school. The kids started finding dog poop on the playground and that was the problem they felt passionately about. We ended up structuring our whole project around the importance of taking care of your pets and stray animals. We raised money for the local animal shelter and the big culminating project was creating a brochure for kids on how to take care of your pets, which we brought to the local animal shelter. It was this beautiful scene and it came organically from the kids.

What are some of the other projects your students dreamed up?

Another year, when I was teaching first grade, I had some students who were really upset because kids on the playground kept killing spiders. They were devastated. They were so upset. They thought it was horrible. Some of that came from me because whenever we would find any bugs or spiders in the classroom, we never killed them. We would just capture them and bring them outside. When they told me, I was like, "Ooh, it sounds like we have a problem, kids." We ended up creating posters with information about how beneficial spiders are and how they don't really hurt people. We had a guest speaker who came in with a tarantula and all these crazy spiders and it was the coolest thing for first graders to see. I always feel like the difference with little kids is you have to be more teacher directed at first so they can understand the process. And then once they do, you kind of have to allow yourself to sit back and see what happens.

How do you use storytelling to help students learn?

At the beginning of kindergarten, a lot of what we do is called emergent storytelling. When they come in, most kids cannot read conventionally. Like, they can't actually decode and read the words, but they can tell stories. And so there are certain books that are considered emergent stories. For example, "The Very Hungry Caterpillar" is an emergent story. Once you read it to them and they hear it two or three times, then they can start telling it themselves in different ways. Sometimes we would make puppets and retell the story using their puppets. Sometimes I would have them make a storyboard where they would paint the background. Then, they're really talking about setting and looking at the details so they can tell the story in front of the storyboard themselves. I've even said, "Let's make a movie!" There are tons of different ways that you can do it. Meanwhile, we are doing alphabet work and sound work. So, you can ask things like, "Oh, my gosh, do you see a word on that page?" And they say, "I think that might be *caterpillar*." That's when they start connecting the words on the page to telling the story.

What about play? Can play be useful in achieving learning outcomes?

Let's be honest, play is the work of kids. It's a struggle because depending on where you work and how the district or the administration views play, you might have to almost hide it in your curriculum. "Oh, so you're saying I can only have the kids play for 30 minutes a day? Well, let's do a meaningful project that's playful and engaging." That's one of the things I love about project-based learning; it's playful. It's almost a workaround, right? The sky's the limit.

How do you encourage meaningful play and what does it look like?

In my kindergarten classroom, I typically had certain types of activities that were available for what we called "choice time." The whole idea was that you got to make a choice of what you wanted to do. I would try to have different kinds of play activities available. There were always some building activities, like blocks and legos. But then, there was also a dramatic play station. Every four to six weeks, the dramatic play station would change.

Can you give me some examples?

At the beginning of the year, it was directed by me because they didn't even know what it was or how to do it. I would usually start the year with a daycare, which basically meant it was dolls like babies with diapers and clothes and bottles. We'd be talking about empathy and what that means. The kids would be teaching each other how to change a diaper and how to burp a baby. They'd say, "I have a baby brother, so I know. Let me show you." It's precious. Usually in January, we'd come to the big turning point. That's when I'd say to the kids, "What do you want the station to be?" Sometimes it would become a veterinary office where we were looking at animals and taking care of animals. Almost every year it was something different. The last year that I was able to do it before COVID, the kids decided that they wanted it to be a Starbucks.

That's adorable. Was it successful?

Yes. It was really cute. We took a field trip to Starbucks and the kids brought little clipboards and they took notes and they took pictures and then we came back and I said, "Okay, well what are all the things that we need to make this into a Starbucks?" They decided we needed a cash register and I said, "Okay. Well then, we have to make one and we better study money. . . ." So then, we're looking at numbers and counting skills during play. They noticed that thing in the back with all the words on it. I told them, "That's the menu, so people know what to order. We better have a menu!" Then, we're writing and we're reading and we're sounding out words on the menu. So they ended up making a little Starbucks and they created almost everything themselves. Of course, the Starbucks ladies were so sweet and they gave us cups and some coffee beans so we could have a "real" coffee shop. We had the little aprons that the kids made.

Do you have any advice for K–2 teachers who want to implement play and project-based learning in their classrooms?

To be honest, not all teachers like the things that I'm describing to you. Play can be a little chaotic, right? Some people want quiet and they want everyone sitting in their seats. One of the things that I try to do when I present and when I coach people is show them all this cool stuff that I'm telling you about. But, when I show them pictures and videos, I also say, "Okay, this is amazing. Right? And you want to do this, right?" If the answer is yes, I tell them the truth: "Well, it's gonna be loud. It's gonna be messy. It's gonna take time. This isn't gonna happen in a day, and in the end, it will be worth it."

Chapter 13

Conclusion

In the process of editing this book, I met weekly with Jim Lang, author of the original *Small Teaching*. I had come to look forward to our Monday afternoon Zoom sessions. Jim has an innate gift for providing feedback in the gentle and encouraging manner to which I am most receptive. It wasn't all citations and commas. Sometimes it was fun. On Monday, October 11, we decided on the cover design. On Monday, October 18, we discussed our endorser wish list. Then, on Monday, October 25, for the first time ever, Jim didn't show. I thought it was odd that Jim would miss a meeting, but at the time, I was preoccupied.

When people ask if my husband and I are planning to start a family, he likes to wink and say, "We're in the market." It always gets a laugh and avoids the awkward alternative of me barking back something like, "WE ARE TRYING, OKAY? Mind your own business!"

Anyways, in the midst of "trying" I had gotten into the habit of taking a monthly pregnancy test. On October 18, I got home from school, peed on the stick, set it on the back of the toilet, and promptly forgot. At-home tests take about five minutes to formulate a result and by October, I had gotten enough negatives that I no longer bothered waiting around to witness my fate.

Imagine my surprise, when my husband emerged from the bathroom hours later looking like he had tangoed with a ghost. "What does it mean if it says 'pregnant'?" he asked me, brandishing the plastic stick like a magic wand.

"It means I'm pregnant," I told him.

"There's not supposed to be a plus or a minus or something?" he asked.

I shook my head, no. We had a big group hug with our golden retriever, danced around the living room, and submerged ourselves in the filmy haze of new baby bliss.

Jim missed another meeting on Monday, October 25, and then again on November 1. If I'm being honest, I was too absorbed in the awe of my pregnant body to feel overly worried. I thought maybe the universe had sensed I needed a break from editing to focus on this new stage of life. As Princeton Professor of Psychology Tania Lombrozo's research shows in Chapter 8, storytelling helps us extract order and regularity from situations that might otherwise feel unsettling. I told myself a sensible story, assuming Jim was just busy with his own writing project and would get back to me as soon as he could. I zipped him a short email with the subject line "Checking In." Still nothing.

On November 8, I finally heard back—but not from Jim. The email that arrived from his account read as follows:

Sarah,

This is Jim's brother Tom unfortunately Jim is in the hospital and will be there for some time. We will know more next week and will keep you updated.

Thanks

Tom

At that point, I became concerned.

As my own body began the hard work of assembling a tiny human, Jim's body was breaking down. He had developed a severe case of myocarditis, an inflammation of the heart. One doctor reportedly told him, "You now have a useless pound of muscle sitting where your beating heart used to be." I'm sure that came as a comfort. (Might I suggest a bedside manner simulation exercise like the one discussed in Chapter 9? Just a thought.)

Jim spent months on life support at Tufts Medical Center in Boston, surrounded by his children and his incredible wife, Anne, whom you met in the Introduction to this book. Then, on December 21, Jim underwent a transplant, providing him with a fully functioning heart. I am proud to share that as I write this, he is doing well and in full recovery. I can only hope my own family will possess the love, dedication, and purpose that the Langs have shown over the last few months.

I am so grateful for the guidance and support Jim has given me in my career. He is not only an expert on the science of learning, he is also an unshakable force of light and positivity. The human brain is complex and scientific business, but if there's one thing my research for this book has taught me, it's the importance of self-transcendent purpose. Jim's unwavering dedication to the field of education is a powerful inspiration. As we learned in Chapter 8, cultivating a sense of purpose can happen in three ways: gradual self-discovery, a major life event, or drawing inspiration from someone else's example. In the process of writing this book, Jim provided me with all three of these experiences and he has given me a whole new understanding of what it means to learn something by heart.

References

ABLConnect. (2015). Harvard University. Available from: http://ablconnect.harvard.edu.

Agarwal, P. K., L. D'Antonio, H. L. Roediger, K. B. McDermott, & M. A. McDaniel. (2014, June 3). Classroom-based programs of retrieval practice reduce middle school and high school students' test anxiety. *Journal of Applied Research in Memory and Cognition*, 3(3), pp. 131–139. Available from: https://doi.org/10.1016/j.jarmac.2014.07.002.

Agarwal, P. K., & Roediger, H. L. (2018, November 26). Lessons for learning: How cognitive psychology informs classroom practice. *Kappa Online*. Available from: https://kappanonline.org/agarwal-roediger-lessons-for-learning-how-cognitive-psychology-informs-classroom-practice/ [accessed 22 December 2021].

Agarwal, P., & P. Bain. (2019). *Powerful teaching: Unleash the science of learning*. San Francisco, CA: Jossey-Bass.

Agarwal, P. K., & Agostinelli, A. (2020, March 11). Interleaving in math: A research-based strategy to boost learning. *American Federation of Teachers*. Available from: https://www.aft.org/ae/spring2020/agarwal_agostinelli [accessed 22 December 2021].

Ahrendt, S., Monson, D., & Cramer, K. (2021). Promoting discourse: Fractions on number lines, *Mathematics Teacher: Learning and Teaching PK–12 MTLT*, 114(4), pp. 284–289. Available from: https://pubs.nctm.org/view/journals/mtlt/114/4/article-p284.xml [accessed 22 December 2021].

Allen, C. (2021, August 19). Praising middle school students improves on-task behavior by up to 70%, BYU study finds. *BYU Communications*. Available from: https://news.byu.edu/intellect/praising-middle-school-students-improves-on-task-behavior-by-up-to-70-byu-study-finds.

Ambrose, S., Bridges, M., DiPietro, M., Lovett, M., & Norman, M. (2010). *How learning works: 7 research-based principles for smart teaching.* San Francisco, CA: Jossey-Bass.

Ambrose, S. A., & Lovett, M. C. (2014). Prior knowledge is more than content: Skills and beliefs also impact learning. In V. A. Benassi, C. E. Overson, & C. M. Hakala (Eds.), *Applying science of learning in education: Infusing psychological science into the curriculum,* Society for the Teaching of Psychology, pp. 7–19. Available from: http://www.teachpsych.org/ Resources/Documents/ebooks/ asle2014.pdf.

American Psychological Association. (2022a). *APA.* Available from: https://www.apa.org/education-career/k12/violence-educators.pdf.

American Psychological Association. (2022b, March 17). Teachers, other school personnel, experience violence, threats, harassment during pandemic. Press release. Available from: https://www.apa.org/news/ press/releases/2022/03/school-staff-violence-pandemic.

Anderson, C. (personal communication, July 14, 2021).

Anderson, L., et al. (2000). *A taxonomy for learning, teaching, and assessing: A revision of Bloom's taxonomy of educational objectives.* New York: Pearson.

Angelo, T. A., & Cross, K. P. (1993). *Classroom assessment techniques: A handbook for college teachers.* San Francisco, CA: Jossey-Bass.

Atkinson, R. K., Renkl, A., & Merrill, M. M. (2003). Transitioning from studying examples to solving problems: Effects of self-explanation prompts and fading worked out steps. *Journal of Educational Psychology,* 95(4), pp. 774–783.

Bachman, R. (2017, March 21). How close do you need to be to your gym? *WSJ.* Available from: https://www.wsj.com/articles/how-close-do-you-need-to-be-to-your-gym-1490111186 [accessed 3 January 2022].

Bain, K. (2004). *What the best college teachers do.* Cambridge, MA: Harvard University Press.

Banerjee, A., & Duflo, E. (2011). *Poor economics: A radical rethinking of the way to fight global poverty.* New York: PublicAffairs.

Banning, M. (2004). The think aloud approach as an educational tool to develop and assess clinical reasoning in undergraduate students. *Nurse Education Today*, 28, pp. 8–14.

Barshay, J. (2020, February 3). The science of talking in class. *The Hechinger Report*. Available from: https://hechingerreport.org/the-science-of-talking-in-class/ [accessed 22 December 2021].

Bauerlein, M. (2020). The Rediscovery of Curriculum. *Academic Questions*, 33(1), pp. 120+. Available from: https://link.gale.com/apps/doc/A616359012/GPS?u=mlin_c_burnms&sid=bookmark-GPS&xid=e8763091.

Bean, J. C. (2011). *Engaging ideas: The professor's guide to integrating writing, critical thinking, and active learning in the classroom*. San Francisco: Jossey-Bass.

Beers, K. (2003). *When kids can't read, what teachers can do: A guide for teachers, 6–12*. Portsmouth, NH: Heinemann.

Beers, K., & Probst, R. (2012). *Notice & Note*. New York: Heinemann.

Beesley, A. D., & Apthorp, H. S. (Eds.) (2010, November 30). Classroom instruction that works. In *McRel*. Available from: https://files.eric.ed.gov/fulltext/ED543521.pdf

Benenson, S. (personal communication, May 15, 2021).

Bercume, J. (personal communication, January 11, 2022).

Birsen, D., and D. Kaya-Tosun. (2020). An effective method in improving social skills: Literature circles. *International Journal of Educational Methodology*, 6(1), pp. 199–206.

Blazer, A. (2014). Student summaries of class sessions. *Teaching Theology and Religion*, 17(4), p. 344.

Bloom, K. C., & Shuell, T. J. (1981). Effects of massed and distributed practice on the learning and retention of second-language vocabulary. *Journal of Educational Research*, 74(4), pp. 245–248.

Bowen, J. (2012). *Teaching naked: How moving technology out of your college classroom will improve student learning*. San Francisco: Jossey-Bass.

Boyd, L. (personal communication, August 12, 2021).

Braund, H., & Timmons, K. (2021). Operationalization of self-regulation in the early years: comparing policy with theoretical underpinnings. *International Journal of Child Care and Education Policy*, 15(1). Available from: https://link.gale.com/apps/doc/A670619064/GPS?u=mlin_c_burnms&sid=bookmark-GPS&xid=7ebb8556.

Brown, P. C., Roediger, H. L., & McDaniel, M. A. (2014). *Make it stick: The science of successful learning*. Cambridge, MA: Harvard University Press.

Bruff, D. (2009). *Teaching with classroom response systems: Creative active learning environments*. San Francisco: Jossey-Bass.

Burks, J. (personal communication, December 12, 2021).

Butin, D. (2006). Future directions for service learning in higher education. *International Journal of Teaching and Learning in Higher Education*, 18(1), pp. 1–4.

Caldarella, P., Larsen, R. A. A., Williams, L., & Wills, H. P. (2021). Effects of middle school teachers' praise-to-reprimand ratios on students' classroom behavior. *Journal of Positive Behavior Interventions*. Available from: https://doi.org/10.1177/10983007211035185.

Canuel, R. (personal communication, July 12, 2018).

Cardenas, A. (2021, October 31). Make units more inspiring with vision boards. *Cult of Pedagogy*. Available from: https://www.cultofpedagogy.com/vision-boards/ [accessed 22 December 2021].

Carey, B. (2014a). *How we learn: The surprising truth about when, where, and why it happens*. New York: Random House.

Carey, B. (2014b, September 4). Why flunking exams is actually a good thing. *New York Times*. Available from: http://www.nytimes.com/2014/09/07/magazine/why-flunking-exams-isactually-a-good-thing.html.

Carnes, M. (2014). *Minds on fire: How role-immersion games transform college*. Cambridge, MA: Harvard University Press.

Carpenter, S. K., & Mueller, F. E. (2013). The effects of interleaving versus blocking on foreign language pronunciation learning. *Memory and Cognition*, 41(5), pp. 671–682.

Cavanagh, S. (2016). *The spark of learning: Energizing the college classroom with the science of emotion.* Morgantown, WV: West Virginia University Press.

Chambliss, D. F., & Takacs, C. J. (2014). *How college works.* Cambridge, MA: Harvard University Press.

Chi, M. T. H., Bassok, M., Lewis, M. W., Reimann, P., & Glaser, R. (1989). Self-explanations: How students study and use examples in learning to solve problems. *Cognitive Science*, 13, pp. 145–182.

Chiu, J., & Chi, M. T. H. (2014). Supporting self-explanation in the classroom. In V. A. Benassi, C. E. Overson, & C. M. Hakala (Eds.), *Applying science of learning in education: Infusing psychological science into the curriculum*, pp. 91–103. Available from http:// www.teachpsych.org/ Resources/Documents/ebooks/asle2014.pdf.

Cornelius, T. L., & Owen-DeSchryver, J. (2008). Differential effects of full and partial notes on learning outcomes and attendance. *Teaching of Psychology*, 35, pp. 6–12.

Dickson, B., & Housiaux, A. (2021). *Feedback in Practice: Research for Teachers.* Available from https://tanginstitute.andover.edu/files/Feedback-in-Practice.pdf.

Donahue, D. (personal communication, April 15, 2021).

Doyle, C. (personal communication, October 14, 2021).

Duckworth, A. (2016). *Grit: The power of passion and perseverance.* Scribner/ Simon & Schuster.

du Sautoy, M. (2019). *The creativity code: How AI is learning to write, paint and think.* N.p.: Cambridge, MA: Belknap Press.

Dweck, C. (2008). *Mindset: The New Psychology of Success.* New York: Ballantine.

English Language Arts Standards. (n.d.). In *Common Core State Standards Initiative.* Available from: http://www.corestandards.org/ ELA-Literacy/CCRA/SL/.

Ebersbach, M., Feierabend, M., & Nazari, K. B. B. (2020). Comparing the effects of generating questions, testing, and restudying on students' long-term recall in university learning. *Applied Cognitive Psychology*, 34(3), pp. 724–736. Available from: https://doi.org/10.1002/acp.3639.

Facing History and Ourselves. Available from: https://www.facing-history.org/.

FAQs. (2021). In *Next Generation Science Standards*. Available from: https://www.nextgenscience.org/faqs#Purpose.

Flannery, M. E. (2021). The science of learning. *NEA*. Available from: https://www.nea.org/advocating-for-change/new-from-nea/science-learning [accessed 3 January 2022].

Forkey, H. (personal communication, May 24, 2020).

Frayer, D., Frederick, W. C., & Klausmeier, H. J. (1969). *A schema for testing the level of cognitive mastery*. Madison, WI: Wisconsin Center for Education Research.

Gawande, A. (2010). *The checklist manifesto: How to get things right*. United States: Henry Holt and Company.

German, Susan. (2018). Using models to explain their thinking. *Science Scope*, 41(8), pp. 26+. In *Context: Science*. Available from: link.gale.com/apps/doc/A535300682/GPS?u=mlin_c_burnms&sid=bookmark-GPS&xid=a7704082 [accessed 1 July 2021].

Gladwell, M. (2008). *Outliers: The Story of Success*. New York: Little, Brown and Co.

Gladwell, M. (2013, August 21). Complexity and the ten-thousand-hour rule. *The New Yorker*. Available from: https://www.newyorker.com/sports/sporting-scene/complexity-and-the-ten-thousand-hour-rule.

Gokce, A., Zinchenko, A., Annac, E., Conci, M., & Geyer, T. (2021). Affective modulation of working memory maintenance: The role of positive and negative emotions. *Advances in Cognitive Psychology*, 17(2), pp. 107+. Available from: https://link.gale.com/apps/doc/A667422177/GPS?u=mlin_c_burnms&sid=bookmark-GPS&xid=35690a08.

Google for Education teaching resources. In *To help expand learning for everyone*. Available from: https://edu.google.com/.

Gregory, S. (2014a, October 29). Dynasty! The San Francisco Giants win it all. *Time*. Available from: https://time.com/3547449/san-francisco-giants-world-series-madison-bumgarner/.

Gregory, S. (2014b, October 15). The Kansas City Royals are the future of baseball. *Time*. Available from: https://time.com/3511262/kansas-city-royals-baseball-future/.

Grigg, A. (personal communication, May 4, 2017).

Halpern, M. (personal communication, January 10, 2022).

Harkins Consulting. (2021). In the *KIDS Model*. Available from: https://www.harkinsconsultingllc.com/.

Hedrington, J. (personal communication, December 11, 2021).

Herbst, C. (n.d.). Does the use of bell ringers as formative assessments affect student retention of knowledge in a third grade science classroom? (Master's thesis). Available from: https://nwcommons.nwciowa.edu/cgi/viewcontent.cgi?article=1102&context=education_masters.

Howard, J. (2015). *Discussion in the college classroom: Getting your students engaged and participating in person and online.* San Francisco: Jossey-Bass.

Huang, X., & Reiser, R. A. (2012). The effect of instructional explanations and self-explanation prompts in worked examples on student learning and transfer. *International Journal of Instructional Media, 39*(4), pp. 331+.

Huffmyer, A. S., & Lemus, J. D. (2019). Graduate TA teaching behaviors impact student achievement in a research-based undergraduate science course. *Journal of College Science Teaching, 48*(3), pp. 56+. https://link.gale.com/apps/doc/A566680457/GPS?u=mlin_c_burnms&sid=bookmark-GPS&xid=cf46e0c9.

Huner, S. B. (2021, May). Examining the Background of Student Questions. *HAYEF: Journal of Education, 18*(2), pp. 102–115.

Igel, C., T. Clemons, & H. Apthorp. (2010, November 30). Classroom instruction that works, Second Edition: Research Report (D. Andrea & H.S. Apthorp (Eds.). Mid-continent Research for Education and Learning. In *McRel*. Available from: https://eric.ed.gov/?id=543521.

Jacoby, B., & Howard, J. (2014). *Service-learning essentials: Questions, answers, and lessons learned.* San Francisco: Jossey-Bass.

K–12 Service Learning Standards. (n.d.). *National Youth Leadership Council.* Available from https://www.nylc.org/page/standards.

Keys to Literacy. (2021). In *Comprehension.* Available from: https://keys-toliteracy.com/.

Khanna, M. M., Badura Brack, A. S., & Finken, L. L. (2013). Short-and long-term effects of cumulative finals on student learning. *Teaching of Psychology*, 40(3), pp. 175–182.

Kornell, N., Jenson Hayes, M., & Bjork, R. A. (2009). Unsuccessful retrieval attempts enhance subsequent learning. *Journal of Experimental Psychology: Learning, Memory, and Cognition*, 35(4), pp. 989–998.

Krathwohl, D. R., & Bloom, B. S. *A taxonomy for learning, teaching, and assessing: A revision of Bloom's taxonomy of educational objectives* (complete ed.). New York: Longman, 2001.

Kray, L. J., & Haselhuhn, M. P. (2007). Implicit negotiation beliefs and performance: Experimental and longitudinal evidence. *Journal of Personality and Social Psychology*, 93(1), pp. 9–64.

Krosoczka, J. (personal communication, May 25, 2017).

LaHair, B. (personal communication, November 22, 2021).

Lang, J. (2013). *Cheating lessons: Learning from academic dishonesty.* Cambridge, MA: Harvard University Press.

Lang, J. (2014, August 25). How students learn from games. *Chronicle of Higher Education.* Available from: http://chronicle.com/article/How-Students-Learn-FromGames/148445/.

Lang, J. (2016). *Small teaching: Everyday lessons from the science of learning.* San Francisco: Jossey-Bass.

Langer, E. J. (1997). *The power of mindful learning.* Cambridge, MA: DaCapo.

Leslie, Ian. (2015). *Curious: The desire to know and why your future depends upon it.* New York: Basic Books.

Lemov, D. (2010). *Teach like a champion: 49 techniques that put students on the path to college.* San Francisco: Jossey-Bass.

Livers, S. D., & Bennett, V. M. (2021). Planning Pitfalls: Considerations for Decision-Making, *Mathematics Teacher: Learning and Teaching*

PK–12 MTLT, 114(4), pp. 306–311. Available from: https://pubs.nctm.org/view/journals/mtlt/114/4/article-p306.xml [accessed 27 December 2021].

Loewus, L. (2021, May 4). Why teachers leave—or don't: A look at the numbers. In *EducationWeek*. (1991). *Responses to literature*. Newark, DE: International Reading Association. Available from: https://www.edweek.org/teaching-leternational Reading Association.

Marshall, K. The *Marshall Memo*. Available from: https://marshallmemo.com/.

Massachusetts Ranks Second on Quality Counts Annual Report Card. (2019, September 3). *Education Week*. Available from: https://www.edweek.org/policy-politics/massachusetts-ranks-second-on-quality-counts-annual-report-card/2019/09 [accessed 22 December 2021].

McCluster, D. (personal communication, August 4, 2019).

McDonnell, J. S., & Roediger, H. L. (2018). Improving learning in education. *Psynopsis*, pp. 19–21.

McTighe, J.. *Understanding by Design*. (2016). Available from: https://www.jaymctighe.com/wp-content/uploads/2018/06/Jays-slides-6.29.18.pdf.

Metz, Steve. (2019). More than a game. *The Science Teacher*, 86(7), p. 6. In *Context: Science*. Available from: link.gale.com/apps/doc/A578047661/GPS?u=mlin_c_burnms&sid=bookmark-GPS&xid=2955055b [accessed 1 July 2021].

Miller, M. (2011). What college teachers should know about memory: A perspective from cognitive psychology. *College Teaching*, 59, pp. 117–122.

Miller, M. (2014). *Minds online: Teaching effectively with technology*. Cambridge, MA: Harvard University Press.

Morris, P., Gruneberg, M., Sykes, R., & Merrick, A. (1981). Football knowledge and the acquisition of new results. *British Journal of Psychology*, 72(4), pp. 479–483.

Moss, J., & McBaine, A. (Producer). (2020). *Boys State* [Motion picture]. Apple.

Mueller, C. M., & Dweck, C. S. (1998). Praise for intelligence can undermine children's motivation and performance. *Journal of Personality and Social Psychology*, 75(1), pp. 33–52. Available from: https://doi.org/10.1037/0022-3514.75.1.33.

Murphy, M. (2014a, October 16). *A study of mindsets in organizations.* Indiana State University.

Murphy, M. (2014b, October 15). How students perceive faculty mindsets. Email to the author.

National Research Council. (2000). *How People Learn: Brain, Mind, Experience, and School: Expanded Edition.* Washington, DC: The National Academies Press. Available from: https://doi.org/10.17226/9853.

Nelson, L. (2010). *Teaching at its best: A research-based resource for college instructors* (5th ed.). San Francisco: Jossey-Bass.

Ness, M. (2018, January–February). Reading with training wheels: Modeling metacognitive process using think-aloud. *Literacy Today*, 35(4), pp. 32+. Available from: https://link.gale.com/apps/doc/A525404234/GPS?u=mlin_c_burnms&sid=bookmark-GPS&xid=dae78e1d.

Norman, L. (personal communication, September 7, 2021).

Nosek, E. (personal communication, November 7, 2019).

Novak, J. D. & A. J. Cañas, A. J. (2008). The theory underlying concept maps and how to construct and use them. *Wayback Machine.* Available from: https://web.archive.org/web/20170614211207/http://cmap.ihmc.us/docs/pdf/TheoryUnderlyingConceptMaps.pdf [accessed 22 December 2021].

NSRF Protocols and Activities . . . from A to Z (n.d.). In *National School Reform Faculty.* Available from: https://nsrfharmony.org/protocols/.

Oakley, B., EdD, B. R., & Sejnowski, T.J. (2021). *Uncommon Sense Teaching: Practical Insights in Brain Science to Help Students Learn.* New York: TarcherPerigee.

O'Donnell, M. (personal communication, November 29, 2021).

Ogan, A., Aleven, V., & Jones, C. (2009). Advancing development of intercultural competence through supporting predictions in narrative video. *International Journal of Artificial Intelligence in Education*, 19(3), pp. 267–288.

Oslington, G., Mulligan, J., & Van Bergen, P. (2020). Third-graders' predictive reasoning strategies. *Educational Studies in Mathematics*, 104(1), pp. 5+. Available from: https://link.gale.com/apps/doc/A624995700/PROF?u=mlin_c_burnms&sid=bookmark-PROF&xid=34f3cb69.

Uner, O. & Roediger III, H. L. (2018). "Are encoding/retrieval interactions in recall driven by remembering, knowing, or both?" *Journal of Memory and Language*, 103, pp. 44–57. Available from http://psychnet.wustl.edu/memory/wp-content/uploads/2018/11/Uner-Roediger-2018-JML.pdf

Palacio, R. J. (2016). *365 days of wonder: Mr. Browne's precepts*. New York: Knopf Books for Young Readers.

Paunesku, D., Walton, G. M., Romero, C., Smith, E. N., Yeager, D. S., & Dweck, C. S. (2015, April 10). Mind-set interventions are a scalable treatment for academic underachievement. *Psychological Science*, pp. 1–10.

Pobieglo, T. (personal communication, November 22, 2021).

Pondiscio, R. (2021). "Knowledge map" your ELA curriculum. *The Thomas B. Fordham Institute*. Available from: https://fordhaminstitute.org/national/commentary/knowledge-map-your-ela-curriculum [accessed 22 December 2021].

Pyc, M. A., Agarwal, P. K., & Roediger III, H. L. (2014). Test-enhanced learning. In V. A. Benassi, C. E. Overson, & C. M. Hakala (Eds.), Applying science of learning in education: Infusing psychological science into the curriculum. *American Psychological Association Society for the Teaching of Psychology*. Available from: http://www.teachpsych.org/Resources/Documents/ebooks/asle2014.pdf.

Reser, D., Simmons, M., Johns, E., Ghaly, A., Quayle, M., Dordevic, A. L., Tare, M., McArdle, A., Willems, J., & Yunkaporta, T. (2021). Australian Aboriginal techniques for memorization: Translation into a medical and allied health education setting. *PLoS ONE*, 16(5), p. e0251710. Available from: https://link.gale.com/apps/doc/A662172416/GPS?u=mlin_c_burnms&sid=bookmark-GPS&xid=61796e04.

Rillero, P., & Padgett, H. (2012). Supporting deep conceptual learning: technology can help educators train students' focus away from rote memorization toward deep conceptual learning by building on prior knowledge and making connections between concepts. *THE Journal* [Technological Horizons in Education], 39(9), pp. 37+. Available from: https://link.gale.com/apps/doc/A323038590/GPS?u=mlin_c_burnms&sid=bookmark-GPS&xid=4e837084.

Robins, R. W., & Pals, J. L. (2002). Implicit self-theories in the academic domain: Implications for goal orientation, attributions, affect, and self-esteem change. *Self and Identity*, 1(4), pp. 313–336.

Roediger III, H. L., & Butler, A. C. (2007). Testing improves long-term retention in a simulated classroom setting. *European Journal of Cognitive Psychology*, 19, pp. 514–527.

Roediger III, H. L., & Karpicke, J. D. (2006). The power of testing memory: Basic research and implications for educational practice. *Perspectives on Psychological Science*, 1, pp. 181–210.

Rogerson, B. (2003). Effectiveness of a daily class progress assessment technique in introductory chemistry. *Journal of Chemical Education*, 80(2), pp. 160–164.

Rohrer, D., & Taylor, K. (2007). The shuffling of mathematics problems improves learning. *Instructional Science*, 35(6), pp. 481–498.

Rowe, M. B. (1986). Wait time: Slowing down may be a way of speeding up! *Journal of Teacher Education*, 37(1), pp. 43–50. Available from: https://doi.org/10.1177/002248718603700110.

Roy, M. (personal communication, September 15, 2019).

Santos, L. (personal communication, September 9, 2021).

Schaeffer, K. (2019, July). About one-in-six U.S. teachers work second jobs—and not just in the summer. *Pew Research Center*. Available from: https://www.pewresearch.org/fact-tank/2019/07/01/about-one-in-six-u-s-teachers-work-second-jobs-and-not-just-in-the-summer/ [accessed 22 December 2021].

Schell, J. (2012, March 15). Peer instruction 101: What is peer instruction? *Turn to Your Neighbor: The Official Peer Instruction Blog.*

Available from: http:// blog.peerinstruction.net/2012/03/15/peer-instruction-101-what-is-peer-instruction/.

Schwartz, D. (personal communication, September 29, 2019).

Schwartz, D. L., Chase, C. C., Oppezzo, M., & Chin, D. B. (2011, November). Practicing versus inventing with contrasting cases: The effects of telling first on learning and transfer. *ResearchGate*. Available from: https://www.researchgate.net/publication/232542083_Practicing_Versus_Inventing_With_Contrasting_Cases_The_Effects_of_Telling_First_on_Learning_and_Transfer [accessed 22 December 2021].

Scutti, S. (2018, January 19). Michael Phelps: "I am extremely thankful that I did not take my life." *CNN*. Available from: https://www.cnn.com/2018/01/19/health/michael-phelps-depression/index.html [accessed 3 January 2022].

Smith, S. (personal communication, November 22, 2021).

Sorenson, A. (2020, January 29). Praising students in a classroom setting has big impact on their behavior. *BYU Communications*. Available from: https://news.byu.edu/intellect/praising-students-in-a-classroom-setting-has-big-impact-on-their-behavior.

Southern Poverty Law Center. (n.d.). *Learning for Justice*. Available from https://www.learningforjustice.org.

Steiner, Elizabeth D., & Woo, A. Job-related stress threatens the teacher supply: Key findings from the 2021 State of the U.S. Teacher Survey." Santa Monica, CA: RAND Corporation. Available from: https://www.rand.org/pubs/research_reports/RRA1108-1.html.

Stockton, F. R. (2006). The Lady, or the Tiger? *Language of Literature*, pp. 593–599. Evanston, IL: McDougall Littell.

Stoddard, Dr. Lisa. (personal communication, October 1, 2015).

Talbert, R. (2014, April 28). Flipped learning skepticism: Is flipped learning just self-teaching? *Chronicle of Higher Education*. Available from: http://chronicle.com/ blognetwork/castingoutnines/2014/04/28/flipped-learning-skepticism-is-flippedlearning-just-self-teaching/.

Thanas, J. (personal communication, November 22, 2021).

Trotto, K. (personal communication, December 10, 2021).

Two-Stage Exam—SALTISE. (2021, January 27). *SALTISE*. Available from: https://www.saltise.ca/resources/strategies/two-stage-exam/ [accessed 22 December 2021].

Vedantam, S. (2021a, June 4). The Story of Stories. *Hidden Brain Media*. Available from: https://hiddenbrain.org/podcast/the-story-of-stories/ [accessed 30 December 2021].

Vedantam, S. (2021b, October 27). You 2.0 Cultivating Your Purpose. *Hidden Brain Media*. Available from: https://hiddenbrain.org/podcast/cultivating-your-purpose/ [accessed 29 December 2021].

Vedantam, S. (2021c, December 2). Work 2.0: Game on! *Hidden Brain Media*. Available from: https://hiddenbrain.org/podcast/work-2-0-game-on/ [accessed 1 January 2022].

Vilen, A., & R. Berger. (2020, April 1). Courageous Conversations for Equity and Agency. *Educational Leadership*. Available from: https://www.ascd.org/el/articles/courageous-conversations-for-equity-and-agency. [accessed 22 December 2021].

Vygotsky, L. S. (1978). *Mind in society: The development of higher psychological processes*. Cambridge, MA: Harvard University Press.

Walsh, W. (personal communication, November 22, 2021).

Washington University. (2021). In *Memory Lab*. Available from: http://psychnet.wustl.edu/memory/.

Weimer, M. (2015, March 18). Using cumulative exams to help students revisit, review, and retain course content. *Faculty Focus*. Available from: http://www.facultyfocus.com/articles/teaching-professor-blog/using-cumulative-exams-help-students-revisitreview-retain-course-content/.

Wiggins, G. P., & McTighe, J. (2005). *Understanding by design* (2nd ed.). Pearson.

Willingham, D. (2014). *Why don't students like school? A cognitive scientist answers questions about how the mind works and what it means for the classroom*. San Francisco: Jossey-Bass.

Willingham, D. T. (2008–2009, Winter). What will improve a student's memory? *American Educator*, pp. 17–25.

Wood, K. D., & Harmon, J. (2020, January–February). More than a single word: Why contextual-based vocabulary approaches are more effective. *Literacy Today*, 37(4), pp. 34+. Available from: https://link.gale.com/apps/doc/A619399801/GPS?u=mlin_c_burnms&sid=bookmark-GPS&xid=19ec2018.

Wormeli, R. (2006). *Fair isn't always equal: Assessing & grading in the differentiated classroom*. Portland, ME: Stenhouse.

Wormeli, R. (2021). *Grit and growth mindset: Deficit thinking?* (3rd ed., Vol. 6), pp. 35–83. N.p.: AMLE Magazine.

Wright, J. (personal communication, November 28, 2021).

Wrzesniewsk, A., Schwartz, B., Cong, X., Kane, M., Omar, A., & Kolditz, T. (2014). Multiple types of motives don't multiply the motivation of West Point cadets. Proceedings of the National Academy of Sciences of the United States of America, 111(30), pp. 10990–10995.

Wulfson, J. (personal communication, September 7, 2021).

Yeager, D., Henderson, M., Paunesku, D., Walton, G., D'Mello, S., Spitzer, B., & Duckworth, A. (2014). Boring but important: A self-transcendent purpose for learning fosters academic self-regulation. *Journal of Personality and Social Psychology*, 107(4), pp. 559–580.

Yuhas, D. (2014, October 2). Curiosity prepares the brain for better learning. *Scientific American*. Available from: http://www.scientificamerican.com/article/curiosityprepares-the-brain-for-better-learning/.

Zull, J. (2002). *The art of changing the brain: Enriching the practice of teaching by exploring the biology of learning*. Sterling, VA: Stylus.

Index